Anything and Everything

Brian Arthur Garber

This book is dedicated to those who thought I should write a book, but especially to those that didn't think I could.

Printed in the United States of America

First Printing, 2015

ISBN-13:
978-0692513859

Cover Created by Kayla Garber

Self Published by Brian Arthur Garber

For more information visit:
www.brianarthurgarber.com

Contents

Heroes Just Aren't What They Used to Be

Growing up, when asked who my favorite superheroes were, I would answer without hesitation my favorite superhero duo, Hunchback and the Fat Kid. They were unique because I believe them to be the only Grandfather and Grandson superhero team. Hunchback was about seventy-six and collected social security, while Fat Kid was twelve, annoying, and loved professional wrestling. Also, Hunchback's back was so hunched over he would sometimes be mistaken for a serving tray at a restaurant.

Oftentimes the duo would face their arch-nemesis, Dr. Pain, whom, in hindsight, I do not believe held a doctorate degree in anything; he just loved to try to rule the world.

One particular story I remember involved Dr. Pain trying to sabotage the Lake Green Elementary School's annual Story of Christmas play. His plan was to show up to the play with a sign that read, "This show sucks and so does Christmas!" While this probably would not stop the play, it would lower the enjoyment level of all the parents sitting in the audience.

The duo just could not let this happen. So, on the day before the play the school's PTA tipped old Hunchback off about Dr. Pain's plan. They found out from his weekly public access show.

The night of the Christmas play, Hunchback and the Fat Kid sat on the left side of the auditorium patiently waiting, when suddenly Dr. Pain walked in holding a rolled up sign. He sat down on the right side of the Lake Green Elementary School Auditorium.

Once all of the parents were seated the principal of the school lowered down from the rafters, and she said, "I hope you will enjoy this presentation of the Story of Christmas, the children have worked very hard on ripping off this great play, and if anyone plans on making a disturbance during the play, get the hell out now!" The last part she yelled in a blood thirsty rage.

A few adults stood up and made their way towards the exit; however, Dr. Pain remained seated chuckling to himself. The principal raised back into the rafters which naturally signaled the beginning of the play. The parents began clapping as the curtains parted to their opposite sides of the stage.

The play goes on without a single hitch until the dramatic boxing scene is about to begin when out of the corners of their eyes our heroes spot Dr. Pain starting to rise out of his seat and unfold his sign.

Fat Kid cries, "Boost me!"

Hunchback stands up; Fat Kid jumps on his flat back then quickly jumps onto the stage as he can hear his grandfather's back creak in pain. Then, from the stage, jumps on top of the villainous Dr. Pain thus knocking him unconscious. One concerned parent calls the police on his cell phone, and the police arrive only minutes later to arrest Dr. Pain.

"Job well done boys" Police Captain Caddywonkus says with a smile as he puts Dr. Pain into the squad car. The local news team arrived at the school to speak with the two heroes.

"So, what is next for our heroes?" one reporter asked.

"We are going to my favorite place to eat." Fat Kid said.

When asked where that was Fat Kid pointed an angry finger at the reporter, said nothing, turned and walked away.

"What did you ask again?" Hunchback said. The reporter repeated the question. "What?" Grandpa Hunchback asked again. The reporter repeated the question again. This went on for several minutes until the news team turned away and left the scene with a befuddled Hunchback left standing in front of the Green Lake Elementary School Auditorium.

As for Dr. Pain he received an eighteen year sentence for disrupting an elementary school event, but he was released after only three months for good behavior.

The moral of this heroic tale is: if someone (in this case an elementary school class) works really hard for something, you should encourage them and be helpful, not disruptive.

Intellectual Conversation

Ronald and Alistair are probably the two smartest people ever to hold a conversation. Both were very successful men in the business world: Ronald was the CEO of a Fortune 500 company, and Alistair was British. What made these two gentlemen very smart was in fact not their doctorate degrees from prestigious universities, but their keen ability to disagree with anything simply by calling it "hogwash".

Now hogwash has been used since the middle ages as the universal disagreer, but what does it actually mean? Theoretically, washing a hog should be a good thing in my opinion, they are factually known as dirty creatures. Well it came to my surprise the answer for this question of where the term "hogwash" came from. I asked countless thousands what they believed the answer to be.

According to several scientists and even more English degree holders, all whom would like to remain anonymous and not real, the term hogwash dates back to the early 1100's to King King, yes the King's last name was King. I had a hard time finding information on King King but I did find a few ways to refinance my mortgage. Turns out, King was the ruler of the lost city of Atlantis in the middle of the Atlantic Ocean.

That was not really hard to find information about which is really surprising given the fact that no one seems to know where the sunken city is, but they seem to have the entire history of it.

Anyways, to get back on track, not the first track about the two guys that we both have forgotten the names of, but the second track about hogwash, King King first used this term after losing a game of Texas Hold'em to his enemy Lord Funk.

King found out Lord Funk cheated, and after his servant/maid/timekeeper was done washing the King's hogs; the King grabbed the back of

Lord Funk's giant afro and slammed his face into the dirty water and yelled in what is to be believed in the first time in history, "Hogwash"! Lord Funk would have his revenge four years later by creating disco, thus killing King King forever.

Sadly enough this would not be the last time that phrase was used. I remember when I was a child reading a story, in I believe the newspaper, about a child and his father. Both the child and his father were riding in a car together driven by Fear; they were rich so they had a driver whose name happened to be Fear. The son pointed out the window and said, "That's hogwash".

His father replied, "That's a factory, son". I do not remember the rest of the story except the child grew up to be a paper shredder at a paper factory in Oklahoma and later in life was a three time lottery winner.

Okay I almost forgot about the two intelligent gentlemen in the beginning of the story. One was from England, and the other collected baseball cards, well they had such a great and intellectual conversation that they could have become rich in knowledge.

An interesting postscript to all of these stories is what happened to Lord Funk. After he created disco, Lord Funk wanted to become even richer so he created hogwash cereal for kids.

The moral of this story is, "Sometimes getting hurt can make you say, "ow!"; sometimes small dogs can do tricks that make you say, "wow!""

Decent Attraction

This story begins in the all too familiar setting of a magnet factory. Two of the employees, Richard and Lonnie, were working on a special project for their boss, Francis. It was three weeks earlier that Francis came to the two men and saddled them with the task of finding out how a person could work in a magnet factory if they had an implanted metal plate. Neither man wanted to volunteer to have a metal plate put in them, so they thought they would have a contest to determine the unlucky participant.

It took them those three weeks to decide to see who could balance a quarter on the tip of their index finger the longest and the loser would have to get a metal plate put into them.

Lonnie said, "I think I will go first and you can time me."

Richard thought for a second and then responded, "Why don't we just go at the same time? That way I don't have to pay someone to tell time for me."

Lonnie reluctantly agreed with his co worker and pulled a quarter out of his pocket, and as per cordiality asked if Richard needed to borrow a quarter. Richard declined and pulled a similar quarter out of his sock.

"This one is my lucky quarter" he said.

All work at the factory ceased, as the workers gathered around to see who the unlucky individual would be. The other workers picked their favorites to win and bet with the foreman as he was standing on a giant ice cube asking to take wagers from his co workers. The foreman waved his hands around cueing to cease wagering on the event that was about to take place, and he skated off of the ice cube to land right next to Lonnie and Richard.

"Now you two understand what is at stake here?" the foreman asked kindly.

Both Lonnie and Richard nodded in agreement. The foreman raised his right arm in the air, "Ok when I drop my arm, you both need to place the quarter on the tip of your finger and balance."

Silence was all that could be heard in the entire magnet factory.

Suddenly, the foreman dropped his right arm, and both of the participants placed their quarters on their fingers. Lonnie's fell off immediately, thus making Richard the winner.

Richard felt bad for Lonnie as he knew what was next for his co worker. The foreman grabbed Lonnie's leg and placed it in a giant vice like machine and turned it on, crushing Lonnie's leg. Since Lonnie was a true warrior and had no fear, he did not make any noise as this happened and he barely shed any tears.

The foreman gave Lonnie a stick so that he could hobble out of the factory and go to the hospital to get his leg repaired with a metal plate in it.

About two months later, Lonnie came back to work at the magnet factory with a slight limp and a metal plate in his repaired left leg. All work at the factory halted yet again as the workers stopped working to give their returning co- worker a standing ovation.

Now the tricky thing about magnet factories is: they must make an equal number of magnets so that they connect instead of repel on account of an uneven number would tear the factory in half.

Richard saw his returning co worker and remembered their task given to them by the head of the factory, Francis, to see how a metal plate would influence the magnets being made at the factory. He called Lonnie over to the department he was working in to see the experiment's results when Lonnie reached his side of the factory.

Lonnie noticed Richard waving him over, and he smiled and started hobbling towards the man who caused him so much pain, but he still considered him a friend.

Once Lonnie reached his destination he said, "How are you, Richard?" to which Richard flipped the on switch to his machine, which happened to create magnets that repel poor Lonnie's metal plate.

Lonnie flew straight into the air and through the ceiling of the factory, and he did not stop until he went into space where there are no magnets. Richard felt a little bad about Lonnie, but he was able to write a five page report as to what happens when a metal plated worker goes to work at a magnet factory.

The moral of this story is: it has been said before that opposites attract, and that could not be more true in a magnet factory.

Jasper the Bowling Cat

I remember a story I once heard about a cat named Jasper, who people claimed was an excellent bowler. He was known for bowling at a bowling alley a few hours away from my house. So one day I decided to see him for myself. It was a cold middle of January when I pulled up to the River Water Bowling Alley. I will never forget how excited I was to see a cat that could not only bowl, but bowl well, from what the reports were saying.

So I made my way inside of the bowling alley to witness what I would consider a miracle; if it was an actual bowling cat. I looked at the photos hanging on the walls to see a team of three human adults and what appeared to be a six foot tall cat standing next to them. There were several photos with the same people pronouncing league champions for both summer and winter leagues going back several years.

The name of the team was the same, *The Alley Cats.*

I walked up to the clerk at the front desk and asked if Jasper the bowling cat was in the building. The clerk laughed a little bit and said, "Oh no. Jasper only bowls during tournament play. You will never see him practicing."

I thought that was a bit odd, but felt the need to satisfy my curiosity, so I asked, "When is the next league match he will be bowling in?"

The clerk pointed at a calendar on the wall which had the next day's date circled on it. I thanked him and left the alley to return to my hotel room.

The next day I woke up with a ton of excitement as I was about to see a six foot tall cat bowl at a bowling alley. I brushed my teeth and got dressed, forgoing a shower in my rush to get back to the bowling alley. When I arrived at the bowling alley I was surprised to see three times as many cars in the parking lot as the previous day, obviously others were curious to

16

see this phenomenon. I was right, there were around fifty people crowding around the lane that Jasper was scheduled to bowl on.

The other three *Alley Cats* had arrived and were signing autographs to their adoring fans. Suddenly, the cheers overwhelmed the music playing from the jukebox as what I saw was a giant six foot tall cat with a bowling bag walk towards his bowling teammates. He brushed off a few autograph seekers, and sat down to remove his bowling ball from his bag. The other team arrived and sat down to talk to Jasper's teammates.

Once the bowling match began, I was surprised to see the other bowlers, both Jasper's teammates and the other team use only one lane. Apparently Jasper would be solely using the other lane. A few employees from the alley walked to Jasper's lane with buckets in their hands. They dumped cat litter in both of the gutters and packed it very tight. Once it was packed to Jasper's specifications he started to bowl. Not a single ball went into the gutter because of the cat litter packed into it.

I was severely disappointed that Jasper was basically a cheater. He bowled several times, all strikes on his cheaters lane, but what surprised me is he did not blink a single time since entering my sight. On one roll he missed one pin to which he let out a huge growl, and I could see it clear as day a hand come from behind the pin and knock it down. The entire crowd started to cheer; I on the other hand had had enough. I said, "Whoa, whoa, whoa. I can see this cat is a cheater, but I am not sure he is actually a cat."

Jasper turned and gave me the same look that he had on his face the first time I saw him. He just pointed at me, and the crowd started to get restless and scared.

I walked up to Jasper and I smacked the side of his head, which to everyone, except for myself's surprise, went flying off onto one of the other lanes. Under the head was a normal looking man, who had a mean look on his face as his secret had been revealed.

The security at the bowling alley, who were also police officers, arrested Jasper on sight and took him to jail. The people in the crowd were upset but understood the consequences of cheating the system.

Jasper, as it turned, out was a former employee of the River Water Bowling Alley named Walter Friendly. He was sentenced to nine years in jail for impersonating a cat, which became a felony in 1993.

The moral of this story is: cats can be friendly, yes, but they can never be good bowlers.

Mommy, Where do Birdbaths Come From?

When I was younger my family moved to an apartment complex. Now for those of you who have ever lived in an apartment complex, or visited one, or even seen a picture of one on a postcard knows the most important rule about surviving: Make Friends Fast!

Luckily I was able to do this because my neighbor, Joshua Barton, liked playing with spy stuff just like me. Sorry I went off track from the story, he actually became a spy and got blown up by an exploding fry-cooker while trying to infiltrate McDonald's to find out what new toys were going into their kid's meals or something like that.

Anyways, I remember a time when he asked his mom the age old question, "Where do birdbaths come from?" When she did not have an answer for him, he became very upset. I heard he actually took her to court to try to divorce her from his life, and he was only like eight or nine years old. Again I apologize for getting off the intended pathway of this story.

On a bright and clear day, Joshua and I decided to go to the most exciting place on Earth, no not an amusement park, the mall, or the sewer, and yes, the sewer is a hilarious place to go, but we went to the library to research birdbaths and their origins. We looked for hours, I even asked one of the librarians, but she said I was talking too loud, and she could not understand me. Frustrated, I wrote what I wanted to ask her on a sheet of paper and gave it to her.

She did not even look at the paper and said, "I can't read." I did not know whether to laugh or cry. Then she said, "Oh that will be ten cents for the paper and pen usage."

I pulled a quarter out of my pocket, balanced it on the tip of my finger, and threw it up in the air and yelled, "Keep the change!" I stormed out of the library with Joshua following me.

On our way out of the library I noticed something to my left, a homeless person sitting down reading a book. "Oh great! A literary bum." Joshua said. I smacked him with an ironic backhand. "Do you not know the poorest people are always wealthy with knowledge?" I took two steps towards the homeless man and asked, "Sir, do you know where birdbaths come from?"

He replied with, "No…but I know what they are made of."

"What are they made of sir?" I asked waiting for a reply intently.

He thought for a second then replied with, "Eggshells, snail shells, burnt orangutan shells, turkey shells, clamshells…." He just kept going on naming random shells so Joshua and I started backing up, but continued to hold eye contact until we got close enough to my car.

We quickly got into my car, and on our way out of the parking lot we drove past the homeless man, and as we did so Joshua rolled down the passenger's side window and threw a three pound bag of ice in the homeless man's general direction smashing both his hopes and his dreams of a better future.

It is common knowledge that ice is the most deadly thing to give to a homeless person. Needless to say I scolded Joshua for his juvenile behavior.

It goes without saying we did not find the origin of the birdbath that fateful day, but as with everyone, it is something that you learn when you become an adult.

The moral of this tale is libraries can be scary, but someday everyone has to face their own fears and not run away from them forever.

How Much Toothpaste Can One Person Eat?

Yes, it is the age old question that has never been answered, attempted many times but never fully answered. Of all of the attempts in recorded history my favorite happens to be by a man named William-Walter "Daisy" Weismann. I had the opportunity to interview this almost champion at the Teeth Cleaning Convention in Sacramento in early 1999.

He was the guest of honor that year so thankfully he accepted my request to interview him, if only I would pay him the low fee of $75. So it was good to see not only did the fame and fortune not go to Mr. Weismann's head but also his ego was not nearly as inflated as the super celebrities of today.

He met me in a secluded room, and he allowed only one pen and one sheet of loose-leave paper. He also limited me to only asking ten questions, and said that each additional question would cost around fifteen dollars. I then said, "What do you mean around fifteen dollars?"

Weismann replied with, "First off that is your first question, second "around fifteen dollars" means twenty-five dollars plus tax."

At this point I knew that I must outsmart him or else I was not going to get to ask any of my journalistic questions. So without hesitation I began with my first question or second if you ask William-Walter, "How far did you get to finishing off an entire tube of toothpaste in one sitting, before you failed?"

He answered with, "About three fourths of the way into the tube." Our conversation went as follows from there:

"Would you care to elaborate?"

"No."

"I think the TEC (Toothpaste Eating Community or Toothpaste Eating Championship depending on what country you live in) deserves an answer, don't you?"

"I really do not think that they care."

"Why not?"

"It is of my opinion that people, especially young people who have their whole lives ahead of them, and older people who have very little left to live for should not occupy their time with eating toothpaste."

"You do know this will send shockwaves throughout the entire TEC?"

"So what, someone needed to speak the truth."

"Do you know how many members of TEC there are in the United States alone?"

"No, and I do not care either."

"There are twenty-seven, and do you know what they will do to you once this interview hits the presses?"

"It does not bother me because I really do not care what they might do."

"Have you ever heard of Morgan Crawford?"

"No, is she famous too?"

"She was the last person who made insidious comments about the TEC, and do you know what happened after that?"

"No, but I do know something you do not."

"What's that?"

"That was your tenth question, so write me out a check for $75, and I will be on my way."

I stood up from my chair, threw the check on the ground as I realized I had just been bested by the best con man in the business who calls himself a celebrity, even though he still could not finish off a whole tube of toothpaste.

Sadly, I would not see him again so that I could exact my revenge on this sinister man; however, several years later riding the train through South Detroit, there was a short stubby man sitting by himself on the other side of the train car, who looked exactly as I pictured what William-Walter Weismann would look like nowadays, but as soon as I saw him the train stopped at a station, and he got off and I stayed on.

Asking that man if he was Weismann was one question that I never got to ask.

The moral of this tale is to always ask questions of both strangers and authority because only good things can come of it.

Walk Softly and Hit Things with a Baseball Bat

Fat Kid was flipping through the three hundred channels on his grandpa's television. He stopped when he saw a baseball game was being broadcast. It happened to be a college baseball game from 1999.

He turned to Hunchback, who was trying to finish the crossword puzzle in the newspaper, and said, "These guys aren't real men," as he was shaking his head in disgust.

Hunchback just kept on trying to figure out what the answer was to 17-across and ignored his grandson.

Suddenly, on the television, the batter hit the next pitch for a homerun, and the crowd in the stands began to cheer loudly; this got Hunchback's attention. He lowered the newspaper and said, "Fat Kid, let's go to a baseball game."

Hunchback picked up the Sports section of the newspaper and said, "Well it looks like there is a game today at 1pm and even better it is senior citizen discount day today!"

Fat Kid could not disappoint his elated grandfather, so he reluctantly agreed to attend the baseball game.

Lance Rivera was thinking about his days as a minor league baseball player, and he was thinking about how he could make a lot of money really fast. He began searching through his closet to see what items he could sell. His search came up empty as all minor league baseball items are worthless, but what he did find was his lucky baseball bat nicknamed "The Bat." It earned this nickname when he hit his one and only homerun in his life in a college baseball game during the 1999 season.

He smiled as he looked over the aluminum bat with a hand written sticker on it that read "The Bat." He came to the realization quickly that he would not play professional baseball anymore, even at the minor league level, because college is the highest level of baseball that an aluminum bat can be used in, and without "The Bat" he would not be able to be a good enough hitter to reach the major league level.

Lance marveled at the sight of "The Bat" for a little while longer, until he came up with a solution to his problems. He knew his job as a greeter at a fresh fish market was not able to pay all of his bills, so he decided he would have to break the law to compete in the game of life.

Hunchback and Fat Kid loaded up the station wagon with enough two liter bottles of soda to last a normal person five years, because Fat Kid might get thirsty on the way to the ballpark. It took the duo thirty minutes to reach the ballpark.

On their way from the parking lot to the box office, a man dressed in a baseball hat and jersey stopped them and said, "If you guys are looking to buy some tickets, I have two seats in the outfield for just forty dollars."

Fat Kid kept his focus on his cell phone as he tried to beat his highest score on *Ninja Fruit Slicer*.

Hunchback looked puzzled for a moment then said, "What about my senior citizen discount?"

The ticket scalper looked confused, but replied, "Yeah, it's close to game time, I can give you a senior citizen discount."

Hunchback cracked a smile for the first time in years as he pulled a fifty dollar bill from his wallet and handed it to the ticket scalper. "As a senior citizen, I'm glad we get so many great deals, we deserve it. Fifty dollars for these two tickets, in this economy, is a steal!"

Hunchback laughed as he took the two tickets and left a bewildered ticket scalper holding the fifty dollar bill.

"Idiot," the ticket scalper mumbled under his breath.

Lance Rivera was holding his favorite bat in his hands as he entered Mike's Hardware and walked to the counter at the front of the store. He was so nervous "The Bat" was shaking in his right hand, but he was determined this would settle his life and put him on the path to a more respectable life.

As he approached the counter a nice woman wearing a nametag that read Amy said, "How can I help you today?"

Lance had a worried look on his face but managed to say, "I want all of the money in the register this is a robbery."

Amy looked alarmed for a moment, and then she squinted to see the words "The Bat" written on Lance's bat. She started to chuckle, then she said, "Two things: we are only allowed to be robbed by someone carrying an official major league baseball bat, and second, you are Lance Rivera, who hit that homerun back in 99."

Lance was completely distraught as he lowered his bat to his side.

"What ever happened to you? After college it seems like your career went nowhere," Amy asked curiously.

Lance turned around and with a sense of sadness walked out of the hardware store empty handed. He did however; know what the next step to his operation was to be: steal a major league level baseball bat to rob another business.

The seats to the game that Hunchback got ripped off on turned out to be great seats. They were located just behind the home team's dugout on the third base line.The game was about to begin and Fat Kid had just finished his fourth order of fresh and hot nachos and onion rings.

As the umpire yelled "Play Ball!" Fat Kid dipped one of the onion rings into a pile of bar-b-que sauce.

Fat Kid said out loud, "Man, I love me some baseball!" as the onion ring grease stained his shirt.

Lance Rivera drove his old pick up truck to the parking lot of the baseball stadium. He put the parking brake on for safety reasons and exited the truck. Lance made his way to the box office to get a ticket to get in to the first professional league baseball game he had attended in many years.

He asked the ticket seller, "How much is it to get into today's game, cheapest ticket you have?"

The employee at the box office shook his head and said with a smile, "Gentle sir, the game has already begun, so go ahead on in there and enjoy for free!"

Lance Rivera had a look of bewilderment on his face as he went through the turnstile to enter the ballpark.

The second inning of the game came to a close as the home team increased their lead by one run. An advertisement ran on the electric scoreboard that stated if the home team scored seven or more runs in the game, everyone in the stands wins a free pizza.

Fat Kid started to jump up and down in excitement, but fell back into his seat when he saw the cotton candy vendor make his way to their section. He rose up both of his hands as Hunchback reached into his pocket to find a twenty dollar bill to gain his grandson another snack.

Lance walked out from the concourse of the stadium into the seating area to get a better view on his eventual prize: a professional league baseball bat. His eyes became locked on the home team's dugout as he knew there would be several baseball bats inside. Lance just had to figure out a way to get inside the dugout.

As he walked down the stairs to get closer to the field level, the cotton candy vendor stopped him and said, "Sir, if you are looking to buy some cotton candy, I have some bad news."

Lance just pushed him out of the way and continued on towards his prize. His mind contemplated for a moment if he should just sit down in a seat and hope a batter would accidentally throw his bat into the stands, but he quickly dismissed the idea.

The batter hit the ball right back to the pitcher on the ground and was easily thrown out at first base.

Fat Kid shook his head and said, "These guys stink."

Hunchback was nodding off, which was noticed by the camera man, so he immediately focused his camera on Hunchback sound asleep in the stands. The sound of the uproarious laughter in the stadium was astounding. Fat Kid himself thought it was funny too, but decided to nudge his old grandpa back to being awake.

Lance Rivera hatched his ultimate plan: when the batter on-deck was waiting for his turn to bat, he would take his bat right out of his hands. He smiled at the thought of his devious plan.

The batter walked up to home plate to await his pitches, and an unassuming on-deck batter made his way out of the dugout. Lance spotted the on-deck batter to be his old college roommate and teammate Christopher Bellowdog; he knew this would be his chance to take a bat.

He finally reached the front row in the stadium right behind the on-deck batter's circle. Lance yelled, "Hey Chris!" to which Christopher Bellowdog turned around at the sound of the familiar voice.

Christopher recognized Lance and walked up to him.

Lance said, "This is going to sound really weird but I'm going to need something from you."

Christopher reached into his back pocket and pulled out a stick of bubblegum.

Lance shook his head, "No I need your baseball bat" he was pointing at his old friend's baseball bat.

Christopher replied, "Well I kinda need it."

Lance reached over the barrier in between them and grabbed the bat out of Christopher's hand. Christopher shrugged and walked back to the dugout to get a new baseball bat.

Fat Kid was stunned as he witnessed Lance take the bat right out of Christopher Bellowdog's hands.

He punched the sleeping Hunchback in the arm and said, "Hey I want a free baseball bat too! That's not fair!"

His grandfather slowly awakened and raised his hand, thinking someone was giving out free baseball bats, and in the process dropped his newspaper on the ground.

Lance Rivera was clutching the bat with both of his hands as he was running back up the stairs to make his escape with his newly stolen treasure. He would have made his escape cleanly except for the newspaper that he slipped on while running up the stairs.

Lance fell to the ground as Fat Kid took the bat out of his hands, and in the meantime, Captain Caddywonkus walked up to the downed criminal to arrest him.

"Free bat!" Fat Kid yelled as he held the baseball bat up in the air with both hands. He then noticed Captain Caddywonkus and said, "What's with the getup Cap?"

Captain Caddywonkus was wearing a bright orange disco suit. "I must have gotten the days messed up on the calendar. I thought today was 1970's day, not senior citizen day," Captain Caddywonkus answered. He continued, "You boys did another outstanding job. The man you captured was probably desperate for sports memorabilia."

The stadium security was arresting Lance Rivera. Hunchback leaned over and picked up his stepped on newspaper, there was a footprint right on top of the crossword puzzle.

He promptly ripped the newspaper in half and shouted, "Where is the justice?" To which everyone in the section laughed hysterically.

The moral of this tale is: there is no such thing as one item that will grant you a solution to all

of your problems, unless you are talking about
money, if you have enough money you can
solve any problem.

State of Mind

There once was an old man by the name of Thomas Albright who was cleaning out his garage. His wife was no help to him as she was busy in the house watching *The Dish Cleaning Network*. So, Thomas was pulling a large box off of one of the shelves that he had built by hand. Naturally the shelf was old too, so when he shifted the box to the edge of the shelf it snapped in two and the contents spilt out. Onto the garage floor went his box that was filled with his trophies and many of them broke into pieces, never to be replaced. A few tears started to roll down Thomas Albright's cheeks as he reminisced about winning the trophies that were now broken.

"Yes, younger times, better times," he said solemnly.

In the 1940's and 1950's Thomas had been a champion at putting slogans on coffee mugs. Once, in 1945, just after the Allies won the

Second World War, Thomas wrote "Too hot to handle" on a coffee mug, and that won him the South Texas Championship in Coffee Mug Naming. In fact, Mr. Albright was so famous for his coffee mug naming he even proposed to his wife by handing her a coffee mug that read: "Will you marry me, hot stuff?" It was the talk of the town for years.

Gentlemen would tip their caps to him and ladies would just smile and look away, thinking of the romantic gesture he had concocted. Originally, he had won her heart by giving her a coffee mug that read: "Hot for teacher" when he was working as a janitor for a school that his soon to be wife, June, was teaching at.

Later in Mr. and Mrs. Albright's lives they had two children, Robert and Elizabeth, both of whom were some of the smartest children in the area. Every Christmas, without fail, both children would receive a coffee mug with a slogan such as: "Don't talk to me before my morning hot coffee" or "hot tempered" for example.

He was so treasured in the town of Russoboro that he was even asked to write a column in the newspaper called *Hot Coffee Talk*, where Thomas would review several people's special coffee blends. The ironic thing is Thomas Albright did not like to drink coffee, on account of his taste buds being melted off from drinking too hot of coffee. He just happened to be famous for writing slogans on coffee mugs. His wife, June, would drink the coffee and tell him how it tasted so he could write up a review.

June Albright heard the loud noise coming from the garage and managed to lift herself off of the couch to rush to the garage to make sure her husband was alright. When she opened the door, she saw Thomas crying and trying to pick up the pieces to his broken trophies. The only thing June thought to do was hug him and tell him everything would be alright.

The moral of this story is: no matter how much you love to think of the past, the present is where those that are most important are waiting for you.

This is the Jungle, be Cautious

Professional television watchers are a rare thing in this day and age; however, as many will remember back in the 1960's it was much more common, on account of television being a new medium of entertainment. That is why this story is about a man named Ray Harris Jr., who had the rare profession of being a professional television watcher.

In fact, Ray Harris Jr., according to reports of people who filed taxes in the year 2015, was the only person with the occupation "professional television watcher".

Not only had Ray received a Master's Degree from a prestigious university in television watching, but he also had the added advantage of his father, Ray Harris Sr. being one of the first members of the "Television Watching Crew" in the 1960's.

Every day of his boring life Ray Harris Jr.'s routine was the same: he would first pour himself a bowl of ice cold cereal from his freezer with warm milk, then he would sit down on his old brown leather couch, and last, but not least, turn on the television.

He would waste his days watching television shows his entire waking day. Ray was always told by his mother that he had the potential for greatness, but being as lazy as Ray was, he would rather live off of the money that his father made from being one of the original members of the "Television Watching Crew".

The house that he lived in was paid for by his father, and he had no need for a car since he did not leave the house. All of his food was on mail order from Brazil, and had been prepaid for the next fifty-five years, which would in fact be still running long after Ray Harris Jr.'s life had ended; his parents had made sure of that. His boring, uneventful life had been going just the way he planned until one day there was a knock on his door.

Now, one thing that must be understood is: Ray Harris Jr. never had any visitors what so ever, in fact, most of his neighbors believed the house to be empty, except for when Ray had his television turned up too loud at night. Ray was startled by the noise of the loud knock, thinking it was just construction outside he remained settled into his leather couch. Then, another knock came to Ray's front door. He knew that he must react, and react fast.

Ray jumped up from his couch and snuck his way to his front window to see who was knocking on his door. He had seen enough police and spy shows to teach him how to be elusive. He peered out the window to come up empty, as he could not see who was at his door. Then another knock came at the door.

"Three knocks, this must be important" Ray thought to himself.

He began to think of the mystery shows and how answering the door can lead to danger, but he also reminded himself of the commercials of people receiving big checks for opening their front door. So Ray opened his front door to find to his surprise a cheetah standing at his front door. Not just any ordinary cheetah, but a three-legged one named Lt. Dan.

"Hello Ray, have you heard the word of Lt. Dan?" the sly cheetah said.

Ray thought for a second and decided he really needed to shut his front door, but the trickster cheetah slipped one of his paws to the inside of the door, blocking any attempt to shut the front door.

Ray was upset because he knew this would cut into his television watching time for the day, "Look I don't have time for your mystic mumbo-jumbo. I don't want to hear what you have to say, and I don't care what you think about it."

The evil cheetah had a big grin on his face, "Now that is not very nice of you, Ray."

Ray was visibly mad now, "Nice? I don't care about nice, I got TV to watch man!"

Lt. Dan knew this was his time to make a move, "Oh I was just coming over to watch some TV with you. I was sent forward in time by your father to take care of you, and he mentioned how much you loved to watch television."

Ray thought for a moment at the situation that was being presented to him. On the one hand it sounded like a setup, but on the other he had seen so many science fiction television shows in the past, and this just sounded like an adventure waiting to happen.

Ray made the mistake of letting Lt. Dan into his house, at best the crafty cheetah would just steal his wallet, at worst, his soul. As soon as the pair sat down on the couch together it became apparent Lt. Dan was trying to manipulate Ray to his will.

"I want to change the channel," the arch-nemesis of everything good said.

Ray put his foot down, "I will not change the channel, all of my judge shows will be on in a minute."

Lt. Dan knew that he would take every opportunity to get his way with Ray. "Who says that you should support these shows? They feature a judge, and who shall be the one who judges the judges?" Lt. Dan asked.

Ray Harris Jr. just stared at the three legged cheetah blankly obviously not understanding what the cheetah just said. A moment or two passed before he replied, "I don't know I just like them; they tell it like it is."

Lt. Dan, quickly realizing that there was no hope of getting anything out of Ray, because his soul obviously belonged to the television, thought to his plan B. He knew not only did he have to get out of the uncomfortable situation of leaving Ray's house while he is watching television, but his plan B to steal Ray's wallet would begin.

Luck as it always seemed to be was on Lt. Dan's side as a bolt of lightning struck the power lines outside of Ray's home, quickly knocking out his power. The sly cheetah knew that this break would be his chance to make his getaway and take the wallet. Lt. Dan quickly got up from the leather couch and grabbed Ray's wallet off of the end table next to the couch. He made his way out of the door, and disappeared into the night.

Ray Harris Jr. continued to live his life the way he wanted to, and continued his same pattern of day until he died on his birthday at the age of sixty-seven, which also happen to be the day cable television ended.

The lesson to be learned here is: if someone tells you that you should do something, or you would be really good at something, do the opposite of that; it almost always works out better.

Poetry Corner 1

In this portion of the book I will include some poems that I have written over the years. Enjoy them dear reader:

Bartender Says

I do not want any trouble
I hate to burst your bubble
This is your last beer
I will set it right here
Then you will leave on the double

Poor Service

I'm hungry for some food
I don't want to be rude
But where is the waiter
Maybe he is a traitor
That is what I conclude

School Days

There once was a kid who used to rule

Everyone thought he was the best in school

Now he is very old

He cleans all of the mold

Because he is the janitor and is cool

Spitting on the Floor

While studying in a college outside of the Australian outback, student Eddie Gomez was learning the ways of the "Force". No not from the popular science fiction movies, something far more dangerous. The "Force" is what many people call sandpaper. It is as dangerous as it is versatile.

Eddie was minding his own business when he was suddenly confronted by a three legged cheetah named Lt. Dan. The cheetah states, "What are you doing in my backyard?" in his famous French accent.

Eddie replies, "How is this your backyard? Who do you think you are, God?"

"Even better" Lt. Dan counters. "I am the mayor of Wyoming."

Realizing this made more sense than anything Eddie had heard before; he takes the first flight out of Australia. Realizing there are no passengers, besides him, or airline crew for that matter, including a pilot, Eddie begins to think about where the plane may land.

The plane lands twelve hours later on the frozen Hoth-like Antarctica where Eddie Gomez has lived for the past seventeen years, twelve months, and fifty-six days. Since the plane landed safely Eddie decided to devote the rest of his life devoted to Lt. Dan.

A few years later, or should I say eight years and fifty-seven days after their initial encounter, as Eddie was keeping track, the three-legged cheetah pays Eddie a visit. When Lt. Dan pulls up to Eddie's farm, in his 1962 Vickers VA-3 hovercraft, he is tending to his deerelkmoose, which is like a combination of the three animals.

Lt. Dan says, with a twinkle in his eye and a sly grin on his face, "You should not have trusted me." The cheetah bumps Eddie with his hovercraft, and he flies ten feet away landing on a birdseed landmine that kills him instantly from birdseed inhalation. Lt. Dan presses the red button on the control console on the hovercraft which launches him into the night laughing as he leaves Antarctica.

The moral of this story is if you ever meet a three- legged animal that talks to you, you might need help from someone, and maybe, just maybe the Salvation Army can defend you, as it is common knowledge that is what they do with the money given to the volunteer Santa in front of your local shopping mall.

The Value of a Champion Should Never be Questioned

Many people do not realize what it takes to be a champion in life. Of course you would think that would be the ultimate goal for anybody, but most people are just fine with getting by and doing what needs to be done to survive on a daily basis. Fortunately, for the rest of us there are true heroes that show us a future much brighter than our own such as firefighters, police officers, and baseball players.

Overlooked in all of those happens to be the snake catchers, more specifically, beach snake catchers. These brave men and women risk their ankles being snipped by crabs walking along the beach; however, over the past few years snake catchers on the beach have received an increase in their annual budget from the federal government, but still not enough to invest in horses for the catchers to ride.

Instead they are forced to purchase the cheaper alternative to a horse, which happens to be an ostrich. The number of catcher fatalities has dropped from one to zero since the inception of the Ostrich Rider Act.

So, if you one day go to the beach on a sunny day and see a man or woman on the back of an ostrich collecting dangerous snakes off of the sandy beach, please give them a pat on the back, but do not talk to them, they do not like being disrupted. If you want to acknowledge them further than a pat then there is also the Official Ostrich Salute, which, in case you do not have a computer at home is: clap your hands together twice and alternate clapping the bottoms of your foot with your hands. The catchers will greatly appreciate the respectful salute.

The moral of this informative entry is: Even if you see someone doing something ridiculous, they might just be doing their job, so be courteous.

School Bus Bully Danger

Growing up where I did, students were required to ride the big yellow bus to school. From about fifth to seventh grade it was a great time: hanging out with friends, listening to the rock music stations, and playing bingo went on normally each and every morning. The good times ended when a transfer from Jackson Lakes Middle School named Sarah Jolley started to ride the bus with us.

I dreaded going to school every morning due to the fact she was now riding on the bus, because she was known to always cause problems.

One day I remember vividly, Sarah had one of her favorite targets of ridicule in her sights: Doug Wallenbach. Doug was a small kid with freckles and red hair, who also wore glasses, and had a Sesame Street lunchbox that he carried around with him. He also sometimes wore pink ribbons in his hair on Fridays. Due to these factors, it caused him to be ridiculed by Sarah constantly.

Doug sat down in his usual seat directly behind the bus driver.

Sarah moved from her seat in the rear of the bus to sit directly behind poor Doug.

She started the morning off by saying: "Hey Doug, what did your mommy pack you for lunch?"

To which he whimpered: "Ms. Jolley, my mommy packed me a ham sandwich and a piece of Texas Toast."

Not satisfied with his answer, Sarah began to flick the back of Doug's ear with her right middle finger and thumb.

The bus driver, who we all called Mr. Rickey, did not notice what was going on because he had headphones on and was listening to a self help book on tape.

My friends and I decided today was the day that we were going to put a stop to Sarah Jolley's reign of terror. A group of us formulated a plan to completely humiliate Sarah Jolley: we would destroy her credibility.

One of my tech friends named Jack used his phone to research Sarah and her family, and within a few seconds, was able to find out everything he needed to know to stop her. He relayed the information to Wesley and he made the announcement to the entire bus that Sarah Jolley's family owns a turtle farm upstate.

Once that fact was delivered, the entire bus erupted in laughter that visibly shook Sarah to her core. Not only did she stop picking on poor Doug, but she shut down completely and would not talk to anyone for the rest of the day.

The next morning, when Mr. Rickey's bus pulled up to Sarah Jolley's stop, instead of her entering the bus, her father, Richard Jolley stepped up onto the bus.

"I want to know why my daughter is too sad to go to school today!?!" he demanded.

Mr. Rickey looked at him for a second and replied coolly, "She got what was coming to her.

She had been picking on that poor boy with the pink ribbons in his hair." He pointed towards Doug.

Visibly, Richard Jolley's blood pressure began to rise, "Wait until the school board hears about this!" Richard was yelling and pointing at Mr. Rickey.

The bus driver unbuckled his safety belt and stood up from his comfy driver's seat. He raised his right hand and karate chopped Richard Jolley right in the neck, and he stumbled backwards and crumpled to the ground right outside of the bus. Mr. Rickey sat back down in his seat and buckled himself back into it.

He looked up in the rearview mirror and said, "You all didn't see nothing" to which we all nodded silently in agreement to never speak of this incident again.

I remember a few weeks after this event reading in the newspaper that the Jolley family sold the Jolley Family Turtle Ranch for an undisclosed amount. After this incident, we never heard from Sarah Jolley again, as she withdrew from the school in embarrassment.

The bus driver, Mr. Rickey went on to be on the ballot for the School Bus Driver Hall of Fame in Baltimore, Maryland, but he has yet to receive enough votes to be inducted.

The moral of this tale is: no matter how tough you think you may be, there is always someone out there that is just a karate chop away from embarrassing you forever.

Sports are Meant to be Enjoyed

Gambling on sporting events has been in existence for centuries. In fact, sports were believed to have been created for gambling. One of the most popular sports to wager on is boxing. In the early 1900's, there was a boxer by the name of Dennis O'Grady who was known as "The Bow-Tie Skillet". Every time he fought it was just about guaranteed he would win. That is why he is the most wagered on boxer of all-time, even to this day. The reason he was so good was because his nickname was given to him on account of him cooking his opponent a skillet dinner which would make the fighter sick and not want to fight. So half of his victories are forfeits from his opponent being too full of a fine Irish dish.

Don't get me wrong, O'Grady was a good fighter who trained hard and ate a hardy breakfast of cereal and butter, plus he was also always the best dressed fighter because he would wear a suit with a bowtie which made him much more dangerous. Many companies were started from gambling winnings from people who bet on "The Bow-Tie Skillet". Also, many historians believe the Industrial Revolution was started because O'Grady made so many people believe America was the boxing and gambling center of the world.

The moral of this historical tale is: sometimes having a tactical advantage in a fight does not always mean having a physical advantage, and sometimes being a good cook can make you a good fighter.

You Must Not Repeat the Past During the Future

I remember growing up, a couple of years ago, hearing ads on the radio and seeing ads on the television about a repairman who claimed he could fix anything. Naturally around town he became somewhat of a celebrity, because as advertised he could fix anything.

Old man McKenzie turned on his television only to hear the audio, even though the man who could fix anything had fixed it a few years previously. After hitting the top of his television a few times with a frying pan full of oats; in the process getting oats all over the living room, the picture still did not come on. So he opened the back of it up.*

Much to his surprise a beautiful assistant stepped out. He almost had a heart attack not only because the beautiful woman was inside of his television set but also because she was six

67

feet tall, and the television was only nineteen inches when the screen is measured.

Practically the same thing happened to Sandra who lived down the block from me. Her toaster that was recently fixed all of a sudden stopped working, so naturally she unplugged it and pushed down on the toasting button and within five seconds two rabbits came popping out of the top of the toaster. She was more mad than ever because she figured it is going to cost her more money to take care of the two rabbits over the next ten or so years than it would be to buy a new toaster.

Now over the course of a week there was somewhere in the ballpark of twenty people's things that stopped working by this so called "King of Fixing Things". His name, as a I recall, was "The Great Gibbertini". Now why anyone would trust a guy with that name to fix the most precious of your home appliances is still a mystery to me.

I became frustrated with how people were being ripped off by this guy so I did a little bit of research and as it turns out "The Great Gibbertini" is a former magician who used to work for a circus in Wyoming but was fired for leaving the gorilla cage open thus turning every citizen of Wyoming into gorilla chasers for a day. I started to get word out to all of his disgruntled customers who proceeded to form a mob of about one hundred people.

The following weekend we decided to storm the former magician's store to give him what was coming to him. Once we all arrived he came outside of his store and said, "What is the meaning of all this?" all the while twisting his mustache and letting his cape flow in the wind.

"All of the stuff you fixed is now broken." Old man McKenzie said in an angry tone. "We want you to give us all our hard earned money back."

The former magician thought for a second then replied, "I have a better idea." He closed his eyes, reached into his pocket, and pulled out a magic wand and yelled at the top of his lungs, "Abra Cadabra!"

"The Great Gibbertini" slowly opened his eyes expecting to see the crowd of one hundred gone and in another dimension, but they were all still standing there staring at him.

"Grab him!" Sandra yelled to her fellow mob members. Old man McKenzie grabbed the fraud magician from behind and one by one, myself included, punched "The Great Gibbertini" in the stomach. In the process his lunch money got stolen.

The moral of this story is: If you have superpowers, that's fine, but if you don't please don't lie and say you do.

*This first-time author does not condone opening the back of a television set, it is dangerous. One of my friends tried it and he got shocked, his hair still stands straight up to this day ten years later.

Quick, Someone Call the Fisherman Doctor

I remember once reading a story about a person that I once considered being a hero. His name is: Fisherman Doctor Sutterman. I remember reading of his tales of heroism as he was able to teach even the youngest and oldest people how to successfully fish. His biggest adventure came when he was fishing the Old Country Road River out in Oklahoma.

It was during this time that many of the farmers in that area were having their cattle and chickens disappear at night time. After several weeks of investigative work by the town's sheriff, it was discovered that most, if not all, had been taken at night by a giant fish that was a local legend called, Big Sassy Sally.

It was around this time, luckily for the townsfolk, Fisherman Doctor Sutterman was on his vacation in a nearby Oklahoma town. The trick of Fisherman Doctor Sutterman was that he could catch any fish that was in a river, stream, ocean, or any other body of water for that matter. He was a two time world champion in professional fishing, and in his spare time he would work on building better, and better fishing reels.

One of the townsfolk in this small town realized Fisherman Doctor was not too far away after spotting his picture in the newspaper in the *Celebrities in Town* section, which most of the time was blank.

The townsfolk were so upset their cattle and chickens were being eaten that they decided to call a town meeting at the biggest church in town. The sheriff sat at a large table in the front of the pews, which sat all twenty of the farmers in the town, and he was about to take ideas for a plan to stop the cattle and chickens from being eaten.

Different townspeople suggested different things for what might be eating their animals including, "wolves, warthogs, kangaroos, and dogtrout, but that was out of the question because they made too much noise."

After all of the wild conjecture ended, the simple townsman who had picked up the newspaper with Fisherman Doctor Sutterman's picture on it spoke up that it may in fact be the giant fish, Big Sassy Sally that is devouring the cattle and chickens from the farms. This made the most sense to the townspeople, because all of the farms were connected by a giant river called "The Old California River."

The town's sheriff called the operator and was connected to Fisherman Doctor Sutterman's hotel room in the next town over. The sheriff mentioned the situation to him over the phone and within minutes Fisherman Doctor Sutterman was parked next to "The Old California River."

As he exited his pickup truck, the sheriff was there to shake his hand and fill him in on the further details of the situation.

Fisherman Doctor Sutterman knew he would have no trouble catching the fish, as he could catch any fish in any body of water. His calm demeanor and listening attention of the sheriff were key points in allowing the townspeople to instill their trust in the man who would bring to an end the troubles of their farms.

The sheriff gathered five of his best men and sent them on a boat as Fisherman Doctor Sutterman got in his own boat, and they all launched into the river. It was one of the deputies that spotted Big Sassy Sally first, and he became so excited that he began jumping up and down in the boat causing it to flip over and the five deputies traveled down the river and were saved when they were all caught in a fishing net four miles downstream.

Within a matter of minutes, Fisherman Doctor Sutterman caught Big Sassy Sally, and the townspeople cheered and told him he could eat free hamburgers in the town's diner forever. Legend has it Big Sassy Sally is now mounted on the wall in Fisherman Doctor Sutterman's bathroom.

It was tales like these that made me think he was a hero until the one day that I met him. I was walking into a bookstore in Central Florida, when I spotted him exiting the sporting goods store next to the bookstore. I immediately walked over to him, and I thankfully happened to have his fishing guide book from 2003.

I said, "Wow you are Fisherman Doctor Sutterman! Can you please sign my fishing guide book?"

He stopped in his tracks, tilted his hat up and replied, "I'm just a fisherman, kid," and stormed off into the night. I was very disappointed that my once hero turned out to be a jerk.

The moral of this story is: heroic actions can create a hero, but a mean person is still a mean person.

Rock and Roll out of Bed in the Early Morning Can Be Tough

The 1970's Heavy-Metal Supergroup known as *Hate Your Parents* has always been known for their wild antics. For example, one time in January of 1974 they fed a groupie to a white lion. Later in the year, around June, they fed that same White Lion to a giraffe. Now, giraffes are commonly known as not to eat meat, so the three person band had to create a sort of White Lion slushee.

As the years moved along and the group's popularity began to fade, the three members, Chaz, Trazz, and Spazzz thought they should go in a different direction. Chaz, whose real name is Charles Nolife, suggested they turn to, "Folk Jazz New-Alternative Funk Country with a mix of Hip-Hop and R&B." Trazz, whose real name is Trevor Wallacemonsteinbergilli suggested, "How about we quit music altogether and open a fresh fish market in Nigeria?"

Spazzz, whose real name is Spaz said, "How about we become superheroes?" They all agreed, and since their usage of spandex in the 1980's looked strange enough, they decided they were in possession of the right costumes.

After months of these washed up rockers battling shoplifters, bank robbers, and green garden snakes they decided that they needed a super villain team to battle. After watching cartoons, Spazzz told the group they need to attack kangaroos everywhere because they might have concealed weapons in their pouches. Hours later, at the local zoo, the police arrive to find the 70's supergroup in a pen with fifty-six either knocked out cold or dead kangaroos. The band is immediately placed in jail for the rest of their miserable lives.

In the end, this story proves that if the world needs heroes they have firemen to turn to and not washed up rock bands.

The moral of this story does reflect that going to jail for the rest of their lives is probably a better career move than releasing any more albums or, God forbid, solo albums.

All Bets are On!

The day started out as any normal day would for our two heroes, Hunchback and Fat Kid. Fat Kid was sitting on the couch eating turkey sausages watching wrestling, and Hunchback was sitting in his old dusty recliner looking at the newspaper to see what yard sales were going on that weekend. He had his blue highlighter pen in one hand and the folded up newspaper in the other.

After Fat Kid downed several turkey sausages he asked, "Hey Grandpa what are we doing today?"

Hunchback blankly stared at his grandson momentarily. "What we do every Thursday, you keep yourself preoccupied by the television, and I scour through the paper for yard sales for the weekend," Hunchback finally responded while looking back at his yard sale list in the newspaper; he'd circled two so far.

Fat Kid started to shake his head, "Why don't we do something fun, like go to a restaurant, order only water and see how long it takes them to ask us to leave?"

Hunchback climbed out of his recliner, "Why that is the most disrespectful thing I have ever heard you say!" He was very unhappy and loud. Hunchback continued, "Don't you realize how hard they have to work at a restaurant?"

Fat Kid turned away from the television to hear what his Grandpa was ranting about.

"You have underpaid wait staff, cooks, busboys, and so many other people that work very hard just to serve you an honest to goodness great meal. I will not stand for the mistreatment of any human being."

Fat Kid waited until Hunchback was done ranting and said, "How about we go to the zoo?"

His Grandpa shook his head yes and Fat Kid turned off the television and the two heroes were out the door and into Hunchback's station wagon.

"I know how to get there!" Fat Kid said with excitement in his voice.

Hunchback was secretly relieved because he had forgotten how to get to the local zoo.

For the next fifteen minutes, Fat Kid shouted directions to his Grandpa, as Hunchback drove the wood panel sided station wagon down the interstate. They pulled into the parking lot in front of a huge building that had a giant picture of several horses running on it. The two heroes got out of the station wagon and entered the building. Hunchback was slightly confused at the notices posted that children must be at least thirty nine inches tall to enter.

They walked up to the ticket booth where an old lady with a nametag that read "Mary-Sue" sat on a wooden stool. "How can I help y'all?" she asked with a Southern drawl.

"Well my grandson and I would like two admissions to see the animals please" Hunchback responded while smiling.

Mary-Sue had a twinkle in her eye, "Of course admission will be only two dollars for you, and your grandson will be free since he is a youngster."

Hunchback turned to Fat Kid and gave him a thumbs up sign.

"Now would you like to buy a program? They are only one dollar and twenty five cents today, half priced."

Hunchback didn't even need to turn to his grandson to see him nodding his head. "Of course we would like a program," Hunchback said as smoothly as possible.

"Also today is our Thursday matinee special of fifty cent hotdogs, fifty cent sodas, and half off beers," Mary-Sue said with a wink as she traded one of her freshly printed programs for a one dollar bill and a quarter from Hunchback's wallet. "Thank you boys and good luck!" she said as our two heroes made their way inside of the horse track.

Hunchback was confused again as to why she would say, "good luck" if they were just visiting a zoo.

Fat Kid had his nose buried into the days racing program. He seemed to be studying the book when his grandfather asked, "Where are all of the cages? I wouldn't mind seeing if they have a monkey jungle. They are always entertaining to watch."

Fat Kid just nodded until he reached into his pocket and pulled out a five dollar bill and a one dollar bill. He said in his sweetest tone of a grandson, "Grandpa, can you do me a favor?"

Hunchback nodded and said, "Of course, anything."

Fat Kid pointed at a booth that had a bored looking blonde headed woman sat behind it.

"Can you go up to her and say: I would like a trifecta box of the numbers two, three, and six?"

Hunchback looked a bit confused until Fat Kid told him it was for a charity raffle. "Well in that case I would like to donate too, it is very noble of you to give money to those less fortunate than yourself."

Hunchback was very proud of his grandson. He took the money to the window that Fat Kid pointed at earlier and said, "I would like a trifecta box two, three, and six please, and also here is an extra twenty dollars to give to charity."

The woman smiled and accepted the money and handed Hunchback the ticket for the wager on the first race of the day.

"Good luck, sir," the teller, who was named Charity, said.

As Hunchback was walking to his grandson in the lobby a loud bell began ringing, signaling a five minute warning until the first race was to start.

"I think the animals are this way," Fat Kid quickly said as he grabbed his grandfather's arm and led him out of the lobby door and to an open seat that was trackside. "I think we sit here and the trainers parade the animals around," Fat

Kid coyly said as there were trainers leading horses to the stalls to begin the race.

Once all twelve of the horses were in their starting stalls, the track announcer came on over the loud speaker, "Welcome everyone, to the first race of the Thursday matinee! There are twelve very fast horses in this race that should make for an exciting finish! We will begin momentarily."

Hunchback's face lit up, "We are going to see horses race around on this track?"

Fat Kid tried to play it off, "I guess so." He was studying the program to see what future wagers he would trick his grandfather into wagering for him.

The loud blaring starting horn went off and a gun fired as the gates to the horses was lifted. Both Hunchback and the Fat Kid had their eyes glued on the track action.

"Wow, they let people ride on the horses?" Hunchback asked rhetorically. The horses rounded the second turn and Fat Kid stood up and shouted, "Come on two, three, six!" Hunchback was a bit confused but joined in anyway.

As he was standing up to help his grandson cheer on the three horses they crossed the finished line with the six horse, two horse, and three horse coming in first, second, and third.

Fat Kid hugged his grandpa and said, "I won, I won, I won!"

Hunchback did not want to let the opportunity to hug his grandson go by, so he returned the hug. They both were smiling, and once the payoffs were displayed on the scoreboard Fat Kid started swinging his fists wildly into the air. The trifecta paid five hundred and fifty dollars.

Fat Kid pointed at his grandpa, "Ok, you go back to the window and hand that ticket that I had you get and make sure you give the teller some money as well."

Hunchback smiled, "Oh you mean give some money to Charity?"

Fat Kid nodded, "Yeah like five dollars or something."

Hunchback left to return to the lobby and see Charity. "Here you go," he said as he handed her the winning ticket.

Charity smiled and started to pull out several hundred dollar bills and a fifty dollar bill. Hunchback accepted the money with a confused look on his face. He handed Charity the fifty dollar bill back and said, "My grandson said to give this to you."

Charity's face lit up, "Tell your grandson thank you very much!"

Hunchback returned to the seating area to find Fat Kid studying the program for the entries into race number two.

Fat Kid could see the confused look on his grandfather's face, "We won the charity raffle" he said.

Hunchback smiled and handed the money to Fat Kid. As soon as the money was handed over, Fat Kid started to count it. "Hey, I'm fifty dollars short," Fat Kid said with distrust in his voice.

Hunchback smiled, "I gave fifty dollars to Charity. She is such a nice lady. Which reminds me, your mother said she was going to pick you up at three today. We need to get home to beat the rush hour traffic."

Fat Kid began to pout, until his grandfather said, "We will have to come back another day, so you can see some of the other animals."

Fat Kid smiled and thought about how they would go see dogs at the next "zoo".

The moral of this tale is: be nice to everyone you meet, because not only is life too short not to, but also because you may gain a special lucky ability to pick the winners of a race and win some money.

On a Pond Once Frozen

There comes a time in every person's life that they should go out on a boat and explore the sea. While the concept is a novel one, sometimes it is just not realistic. I used to know a boat captain and his name was Willis Raymond. The thing about Willis is that he hated the water, couldn't even swim, in fact. Willis, however, was very wealthy as the boat he owned was a giant pirate ship that he would take tourists on vacation in around the Gulf of Mexico for about two to three hours. He called the boat "The Sea of Eagles". It never made sense to me either.

Willis ran this ship like he was a hardened captain. However, he had a soft heart, except for people who tried to fish off the side of the boat, and he had no tolerance for fishermen. Of course, he always had a parrot on his shoulder but it was a different one each time because as soon as he went outdoors, the parrot would fly away.

One day, he decided that he needed to make drastic changes to his life because he did not like the sea; his true passion was to open a dance club that only played Australian Folk music. He talked to his closest friend on the boat, Jasper, and he asked him what he should do. Jasper thought for a moment and responded, "Why don't you open a dance floor on this very ship, and when people go out on the tours they can enjoy themselves by dancing to that wretched music?"

Without any hesitation Willis Raymond kicked Jasper off the boat, literally, but luckily Jasper landed on a life raft. Willis frowned slightly.

Willis was upset because he knew that his life must not include owning a ship for him to ever be happy. He put an advertisement in the newspaper to see who would want to buy a used pirate ship, and within hours his phone was flooded with calls. The calls ranged from schools, whose mascots were pirates, to fast food restaurants, to baseball managers. The one call that was most promising to Willis was one from Japanese business man Daisuke Fulton.

Mr. Fulton was known as an entrepreneur whose wealth came from the real estate market. Willis answered the call and set a time to meet with Mr. Fulton the following week.

When the following week came Willis was a bit nervous, understandably so, but was ready to sell basically his life style in order to be happy. The two agreed to meet at Willis' favorite restaurant, The Tank of Fish. The Tank of Fish was known worldwide as the go to place for BBQ pork ribs.

The two walked into the restaurant and were seated at a booth, that happened to be right next to the kid's ball pit, so every time Daisuke began to talk a small child would throw a ball at his face, sometimes it would hit, other times not.

Willis wrote down a number on a napkin and pushed it gently in front of Mr. Fulton. "What do you think about this much for the pirate ship?" Willis Raymond asked. Daisuke Fulton nodded his head yes and began to pull out his checkbook. He wrote a check for the amount and handed it across the table to Willis. Willis Raymond immediately stood up and started to do a Texas Two-Step dance, for which he was just as quickly escorted out of the restaurant.

As the security guards were pulling him out, he managed to throw the keys to the lock that held the pirate ship at the marina on the table so Mr. Fulton could have his newly purchased pirate ship.

Willis used the money to buy a pizza and place a down payment on a building to put his dance club.

I wish I could tell you this story has a happy ending and Willis' club was a huge success, but since no one had heard of Australian Folk music before he would have nights where there was not a single person who went to the club. Although, Willis got to do what he loved and was therefore more satisfied with his life.

One silver lining to Willis' situation is that with the way music trends happen, Australian Folk music may one day become the popular thing to listen to, but until that time Willis will just be sitting in his office at the empty club which he called "Kangaroo and Koala Dance Time" as happy as can be.

The moral to this story is: if you do something that you don't like to do, but it pays good money is it worth it? Would you rather do something that you love and not make any money?

Little Mark Camperelli was not having a good day. First, on the way to middle school, the local bullies, Frank and Billy, started to pick on him for wearing cheap glasses, because his parents could not afford to by him fancy glasses. Now, Frank and Billy were known as the town bullies because they would harass anyone who walked down the block in front of the house that they owned.

They were thirty-five years old and unemployed. They said things like, "Look at this poor kid, he probably can't even see out of 'em glasses!" to Mark. They both chuckled after their mean comments and Mark hung his head down in shame as he continued his walk to school.

Once Mark reached school, he heard the late bell ring as he reached the front steps of the Oakridge Middle School. He ran to his home room class, where they normally watched the school news, but when he finally reached his class and plopped down in his seat, the teacher said, "I have a surprise for you all!" All of the students sat straight up in their seats. "I have a surprise calculus test for you all!"

Mark again hung his head down in shame.

As the teacher was passing out the tests he said, "You all have until the end of the *Pledge of Allegiance* to finish or you will fail automatically." There was a giant sigh as the students did not appreciate a surprise test.

Mark knew he was not very good at calculus, and as he heard the final lines of the *Pledge of Allegiance* he knew he had to turn in his test even though it was only half completed.

Mark was not feeling well the rest of the day, so he asked his first period teacher if he could see the nurse. The teacher yelled at him because Mark was, "Derailing his train of thought." Mark got up and left anyway due to feeling ill, he also knew there would be a detention waiting for him when he got back.

Thankfully, the school nurse's schedule was not too busy, and he did not need an appointment. After waiting for just a little bit of time, she called Mark into her mini-hospital.

"What seems to be the matter?" the nurse asked him.

He winced a little in pain and replied, "It feels like a drill is stabbing into my side."

The nurse shrugged her shoulders and said, "I guess you should go home, we don't want any wimps at school today."

Mark cried a little, but made his way to the front office to call his mom. His mom did not answer, so he hung his head in shame again as he made his way out of the front door of the school and his way back home. Mark was smart enough to not cross Frank and Billy's paths to save himself some ridicule so he took a longer but safer route.

On his longer route home, Mark walked behind his house which had a pair of French doors looking out into the backyard. His dog Mr.

Spot saw him walking up to the house from the backyard and got so excited he smashed through the French doors, breaking them in half, but inflicting enough pain into Mr. Spot that it became apparent he may not survive.

Mark immediately jumped into action and picked up Mr. Spot and brought him into the garage. Mark had a bit of a workshop in the garage for building metal objects, such as his poor man's glasses. He knew that to save his best friend's life he must recreate Mr. Spot as part dog and part robot. Mark slaved for hours on his project, even skipping a dinner by his mom of old beans and popcorn kernels, his favorite dinner.

It was early the next morning when Mark had finally finished recreating Mr. Spot as a cyborg dog. He was so proud of his work because his best friend/dog was coming back to life when he flipped a switched in the garage. Mark's day started to turn in his favor as his fear of losing his best friend was quelled.

Mark now had his cyborg best friend, Mr. Spot, in tow as he took what was to be a friendly stroll around the neighborhood. First, he thought, "Wouldn't it be awesome to see new Mr. Spot take on Frank and Billy?"

He smiled at the thought of having the neighborhood bullies defeated by his new robopet.

He turned to the corner and much to his surprise Frank and Billy appeared to be helping old Miss Hairston across the street to get to the market. Mark stopped walking, and Mr. Spot halted by his feet. He thought to himself, "Maybe Frank and Billy have turned over a new leaf?"

Suddenly it became apparent that while the two bullies were helping old Miss Hairston across the street, they were also helping themselves to her pocketbook out of her purse. Mark had had enough of them and decided it was time to intervene. He yelled, "Go get 'em Mr. Spot!" As he finished the last syllable, Mr.

Spot jumped right into action and jumped on top of Miss Hariston, Frank, and Billy. Unfortunately hurting Miss Hairston in the process, but also fortunate for knocking both Frank and Billy out cold.

Miss Hairston was a little bit bruised on her left arm, but had the where with all to call the police. Since they were outside of the town's bank the police were there within minutes. As the police arrived they arrested Frank and Billy, but also Mark and Mr. Spot. Miss Hairston pleaded with the police officers, "No, you must not arrest Mark and Mr. Spot; they saved me from those two bullies."

She was pointing at the unconscious Frank and Billy.

The police officer who was writing a report on the scene stopped writing for a second, "I'm really sorry ma'am but it is illegal to have a robotic pet in this county and as for Mr. Spot, well it is also illegal to be a robotic pet."

The officer looked back down at the pad of paper she was writing the report on. Miss Hairston had a few tears flowing from her eyes as she saw her two new heroes being driven away in squad cars to jail.

The trials were a spectacle unto themselves, as Frank and Billy managed to bully the judge into giving them a lighter sentence of two minutes of community service. The trial of Mark and Mr. Spot was even more ridiculous, as they were both acquitted of any wrongdoing, because they defeated the two bullies.

In the following weeks Mark petitioned and was granted the ability to own a robotic pet on the grounds that Mr. Spot go through obedience class.

The moral of this story is: being a bully is reprehensible, but being an extra tough bully is even worse, even though it may help you in some legal proceedings.

Insights 1: Traffic Jams

I would like to make the announcement that traffic jams are not all bad. Now I'm not saying it's good if you are late to work or to school or the last minute sale on garlic bread at the local grocery store; however, I do not mind a traffic jam if I have no place to go. At this point, you may actually believe that I am crazy, but during a traffic jam, I have a chance to relax, listen to the latest music on the radio, study the surrounding cars for writing material, and of course to do my taxes.

The valuable time sitting in your car waiting to get to your destination cannot be undervalued, as it truly is a time to sit back, relax, and think. It is one of the few times in life that you are forced to think, unless of course you decide to use that time to make a few phone calls, if that is legal in your area. Which I don't mind either because, of course, it is a very important call.

So the next time you are stuck in heavy traffic just think to yourself, now is the time to get some good old- fashioned thinking done. Not only will it spare you the stress that you previously had with a traffic jam, but it also could make that time very productive, and maybe, just maybe you can realize the beauty of traffic jams, unless you are already late.

Plastic Makes the World Go 'Round

Back in my elementary school days, my friends Ronnie, Johnny, Steve, and I loved to watch detective movies. One day, we decided we could be better detectives than the ones we saw on television and in movies, so we formed the Junior Detective Agency.

We had it all planned out: Steve was to be our lead detective, Ronnie and Johnny were going to do the grunt work of door-to-door interviews and paperwork, and I was to be the research expert. This worked out well until we had our first case. We called this first case, "The Missing Ham Sandwich Case".

One day, the four of us were sitting together on the red metal bench at recess right before lunch was to begin. Robert was a kid that nobody liked in the class because of his stupid haircut, and he solemnly walked up to the four of us and said, "I heard you'se guys were in the detectiving business. This true or not?"

His eyes did not leave the floor.

Steve spoke up for us, "I don't know where you got that information, but it is true. We are in the business of finding things."

Robert glanced at Steve and replied, "I have a job for you fellas. How about finding out what happened to my ham sandwich?"

Ok, I thought here comes a big case for us to work on.

"Who made it for you?" Steve asked.

"My mommy," Robert replied.

The four of us laughed, got up from the bench, walked into the cafeteria, and pulled out our credit cards and each bought a ham sandwich, except Steve: he bought two. The four of us walked back to Robert, who hadn't moved from the previous spot, and Steve took the extra ham sandwich and smashed it in Robert's face. "Here you go, you big baby!" he yelled as we all walked away from the scene, and Robert was picking the tomatoes and ham off of his face.

That was our first and last case as the Junior Detective Agency and boy do I miss those days. Oh, and Robert's original ham sandwich was in Mindy's red plastic *Jurassic Park* lunchbox all along.

The moral of this tale from my youth is: if you need help in life, that is fine, don't feel ashamed at all, but please find the right people to help you.

Poetry Corner 2-Free Verse

Work Ethic
I used to work at a store
Every day it seemed to be a bore
Every day it seemed like a chore
I worked there until I was twenty-four
I worked there until I could take no more
It felt like all of my muscles had tore
My mind was worked to the core
Good thing I don't work with iron ore

Traffic Stop
Once while driving I could not stop
Until I got pulled over by a cop
Apparently I didn't see the light on top
I tried to get away but could only hop
Once in jail it was one call to my pop
He got me out of living in the slop
Now I am pushing around a mop
In a local convenience shop

Our Heroes Return!

This warm and sunny afternoon was no different than any other Sunday afternoon as Hunchback and his grandson, The Fat Kid, were sitting on the porch together wasting the day away sipping on freshly squeezed lemonade. Hunchback was sitting in his old rocking chair made by his father one hundred and something years ago, and Fat Kid was sitting in the swing on the porch playing a handheld videogame system.

"Hey Grandpappy get me another lemonade!" Fat Kid yelled as he finished his glass of cold lemonade.

"What?" the dumfounded old man said.

"Aw forget it; I don't know why I waste my time with you." Fat Kid said as he walked through the front door.

Upon his entrance, the television, which was left on because Fat Kid is too lazy to turn it off, and Hunchback was too technologically inept, began to interrupt the scheduled broadcast to give a breaking news report that the First Bank of the United States was being robbed by arch-criminal Peter Excalibur and his henchmen.

The footage showed Excalibur wielding his sword and ordering his men to take the bags they brought with them and fill them up with the bank's money. Peter Excalibur had already robbed three banks in the past month for a total of two-hundred thousand dollars, and sixty-thousand yen, but not understanding that yen was Asian currency, he promptly threw it all away in the trashcan outside the bank.

Fat Kid rushed back out of the house and said, "Load up the station wagon, and let's go!" Hunchback shot out of his rocking chair and threw on his World War II helmet and yelled, "The Nazis are coming for us!" Fat Kid slapped the helmet off of Hunchback's head, grabbed his arm, and led him to the station wagon.

They often had trouble stopping crimes because Fat Kid was not old enough to drive;

therefore, Hunchback had to drive to all of the potential crimes they wished to stop. Hunchback always kept his promise to his late wife, Darlene, to always drive twenty miles per hour under the speed limit. So, often times, the police had already caught the criminal before the two heroes arrived.

Good thing for the bank tellers, Hunchback's cabin was only a couple of blocks away from the bank. So they were there in twenty minutes. The police had Excalibur and his gang blocked in the bank, but there were still ten civilians trapped inside. One of the henchmen, there were three of them total, said. "Oh, no! Hunchback and The Fat Kid are rolling up to the scene."

"These guys are the biggest joke since the one about Pete and RePete in boat fishing." Excalibur replied.

"What's that one like?" the first henchman asked, but before Excalibur could start the other henchmen piped in with, "Don't get him started it is an endless joke."

Outside, Hunchback and Fat Kid were meeting with the officer in charge of the hostage negotiations. "What's the situation?" Fat Kid asked the officer.

"I don't know, I am new here, let me get the captain."

"No need I am already here." A voice from behind the heroes bellowed. They turned to see the captain of the police force, Captain Caddywonkus. "To tell you the truth, Fat Kid, the situation looks bleak and desperate, but it is what it is. Excalibur currently is keeping his hostages at bay with his sword and his armed henchmen. If we don't do something quick I am afraid there may be no hope for the people inside."

"Well we don't want to rush into anything, but desperate times call for desperate measures." Fat Kid stated.

To be continued…I promise it will be in the next few stories.

The moral of this story...is also to be continued

Cookie Thief, Cookie Thief, Cookie Thief!

I remember a time growing up; I think it was the summer of 1997, that the neighborhood was going through what was called the Cookie Crime Wave. During this time, people were afraid to bake cookies in their own homes for they believed they would be snatched by the notorious Cookie Thief of Papasville.

Now, Papasville was not a place that I had heard of growing up, nor have I heard of it since that one notorious summer. I remember vividly my neighbors boarding up their houses just to make sure that the cookies that they baked were going to their children and not the Cookie Thief of Papasville.

Apparently, this guy would break into houses and instead of doing the smart thing and taking jewelry and money, he would take freshly baked cookies, often times hot from the oven, as news reports would say.

One day, my favorite neighbor Janice was cooking up a fresh batch of her neighborhood-wide famous chocolate chip cookies. All of the kids and most of the adults in the neighborhood loved her cookies, and since it was a very large neighborhood, often times she would cook two-hundred to two-hundred and fifty cookies in one batch. Janice was an old woman (estimated to be around seventy years old), but a tough woman, as she was a master of karate. She knew she would be able to defeat the Cookie Thief of Papasville if they were to fight in hand-to-hand combat. Janice knew this batch would be so good that it would have to tempt the Cookie Thief to try to steal them from her.

She pulled the cookies out of the oven and started to set them on a plate for them to cool, when suddenly, she heard the lock on her front door being tampered with. Her heart started to race as she knew a fight was about to commence. Janice hid herself in her pantry while the lock continued to be messed with.

Her front door flew open and there stood the Cookie Thief of Papasville, a short fat bald man with a mean temper and an even meaner appetite for cookies. She froze as she could see through the slats on the pantry door and the Cookie Thief sniffed the air to try to locate the freshly baked cookies. His eyes locked onto the plate with the hot from the oven chocolate chip cookies. They were on the kitchen table.

He scurried into the kitchen to get closer to his prize when the pantry door swiftly opened and out came Janice with a rolling pin in her hand. She swung with all of her might to hit the Cookie Thief, but with his fast reflexes, he grabbed the wooden rolling pin in time, blocking what would be considered a fatal blow.

Janice was surprised as she had not seen someone else with as fast of reflexes as she had; however, the news had failed to report that the Cookie Thief also was a karate expert, thus having extremely fast agility. Janice smiled slightly as she knew this was going to be a good, evenly matched fight.

They fought each other, but since they were both karate experts, they matched each other move for move. Every punch was blocked and every kick was blocked as well. The fight only ended when Janice tripped over her cat, Mr. Puffy Fluffy and fell over.

Seeing his chance to escape the Cookie Thief picked up the plate of chocolate chip cookies, and smashed his way through the kitchen window, getting glass everywhere. Old Janice was only upset that she would have to sweep up broken glass for the next hour, but after that she would be able to find the Cookie Thief fairly easily as she planted a GPS monitor in the batch of cookies just in case the Cookie Thief made off with her cookies.

After a few hours of sweeping up broken glass Janice picked up Mr. Puffy Fluffy and said, "Mr. Puffy Fluffy, it's time we went on a Cookie Thief hunting mission."

The cat meowed in anger.

Janice loaded up her samurai sword and cat into her van. Mr. Puffy Fluffy used his paw to turn on the GPS locator in the center console of the van. Janice waited as the GPS locator found where her cookies had been taken. The address that appeared on the screen was one that was not familiar to her or her cat.

She followed the directions exactly as the GPS system told her to go and she only got lost for about an hour when her and Mr. Puffy Fluffy pulled up to what appeared to be an abandoned warehouse in the dangerous side of town. Janice knew she could not call for backup from the police, because if she did her status of being karate expert would be revoked.

Janice and Mr. Puffy Fluffy snuck their way to the side of the warehouse to get a closer look inside to make sure the Cookie Thief was there. One quick glance by the two in the giant side window of the warehouse revealed the man who had stolen her cookies just hours earlier. Luckily for everyone involved, the plate, which once held many cookies, still had about half of what she cooked up of the delicious chocolate chip cookies.

She pointed for Mr. Puffy Fluffy to go around one side of the warehouse while Janice made her way to the other side. Much to her surprise, the giant gate on the front of the warehouse was completely opened and the light was shining to the outside ground in front of it.

Janice and her cat, Mr. Puffy Fluffy were on either side of the front entrance to the warehouse. Her cat waited for Janice to count to three and they both stormed into the warehouse with the Cookie Thief. The Cookie Thief of Papasville was so startled when he turned to see the two intruders that he dropped the chocolate chip cookie that he was holding and said, "My, my, my what a surprise it is to see you, and your little cat too."

Janice smiled as she knew the battle of her lifetime was about to begin. "You will be even more surprised when I roundhouse kick you into the next century."

The Cookie Thief laughed as even though he had fought the old woman before, the idea of a roundhouse kick delivered by her was laughable. Both of the karate experts got into a fighting stance and their battle was about to begin.

Once again they matched each other punch for punch and kick for kick. The Cookie Thief picked up a wooden picnic table and threw it at Janice to which she countered by smashing it in half with a karate chop. Janice pulled a few salt water taffy pieces out of her pocket and hurled them towards her enemy. The Cookie Thief managed to grab every single piece before they made contact, and he threw them to the floor.

While the two of them were battling each other Mr. Puffy Fluffy started to eat three of the chocolate chip cookies off of the plate on the table. He was chewing very fast when finally he spit out a bunch of cookie dust right into the Cookie Thief's face, blinding him momentarily.

That was enough time, however, for Janice to deliver her promised roundhouse kick to his face, knocking him out cold.

Janice picked up the Cookie Thief of Papasville and placed him in the back of her van. He was still out cold as she drove him across town to the police station. When she walked through the giant double doors of the town's police station, the officers were delighted to see her, thinking she had made some of her famous cookies for them. When she told them she did not have cookies, but did in fact have the Cookie Thief in the back of her van, the officers were disappointed, but only slightly.

After that day's ordeal Janice went on to become even more famous as she created the world's first cat cookies.

The Cookie Thief was put in prison for thirteen years, because it is known as a baker's dozen.

The town's police force ended up donating all of their charity funds to Janice to help her make her cat cookies, with the stipulation that she bring in some of her famous chocolate chip cookies every week.

The moral to be found in this story is: never underestimate someone you are about to do battle with, or you may find yourself on the losing end and in jail.

Christmas 1994

I would have to say the Christmas of 1994 would have to rank as my favorite Christmas on account of the events that transpired that day. You see contrary to many people's Christmas traditions; my family has done things a little bit different. For example, my grandpa would announce that the hunt for the Christmas presents was on to mark the time that my family members must search for our Christmas presents that either he or Santa had hidden throughout the neighborhood.

On this particular year, the surprise that befell upon all of us was that my grandfather had forgotten to get Christmas gifts for anyone; therefore he did not get any. It should be noted however that he is a crafty man, so on Christmas morning of 1994 the announcement came out like it did every year. "I request the presence of all family members, who are participating in Christmas this year!" my grandpa bellowed.

This announcement told all of us it was time to gather around the Christmas tree to receive our directions for finding the Christmas gifts.

Now remember, this year was special because my grandpa had forgotten to get any Christmas presents. "Your clue this year is the color blue. That is all" my grandpa said to a chorus of sighs. "You are all Christmas Dismissed!" That was the signal to us it was time to begin the search for the presents.

On this particular year there was one exception to the people playing the Christmas Search game, and that was my brother as he opted to stay home this year.

So it began. The six of us jumped into my aunt and uncle's van, and were on our way to the open road. My grandpa stayed home and sat in his Christmas Chair, drinking his Christmas Sweet Tea, and smoking his Christmas Cigarettes. My brother stayed home to play video games and drink raspberry soda.

Anyways, the six of us drove by house after house after house in search of where the presents could be. That was until my uncle came up with the great idea, "I'll bet I know where they are." He pointed to one of the department stores that happened to be open on Christmas Day. He quickly did a u-turn, and we pulled into the parking lot of the store. Once we got inside things started to get strange.

Inside the store, we all saw what we perceived to be our Christmas presents. My parents saw tools needed to help repair the garage, my aunt and uncle found the new big screen television they wanted, my grandma found a purse she wanted, and I found the desktop computer that I wanted. I laughed as I strolled by the video game my brother wanted for Christmas. Thinking he would miss out since he did not go with us to complete the search for Christmas presents.

We grabbed a few shopping carts and put all of the items we thought were part of the

Christmas search in them, and we headed out the store. As soon as we got to the van in the parking lot, five sheriffs' patrol cars were there with their lights flashing, blocking in the van.

"Why are you stealing all of this stuff?" the first deputy asked.

My uncle smiled, "Oh no! We are not. These are a part of our Christmas search gifts from my father."

Within minutes the deputies had all of us in handcuffs and against the squad cars. My uncle explained the situation to the officers, and they sent one patrol car back to my house.

A few hours passed us by as the squad car returned with my grandpa in handcuffs. Once they pulled him from the backseat of the car he explained the situation and how he had forgotten to get presents this year and did not know his family would be stealing from a department store. The kind officers let all of us go except my grandpa, as he was hauled off to jail for being a criminal mastermind.

The big surprise this year was when we all returned back to my house; my brother had bought everyone the exact presents that we had all hoped for. It was a great year indeed, and it brought everyone closer together.

My grandpa on the other hand was arrested for being a criminal mastermind, and for that, was sentenced to five years in jail, but he got out after three for good behavior.

The moral of this story is: appearances can be deceptive, but sometimes deception can lie in appearances.

East by Eastwest

This story begins as many adventure stories do, and that is by being on a fast moving train. Super spy Jack Spacer had just finished flying back into the United States from his last mission in Japan. He was now traveling on a high speed train that would take him from California to Texas where he would later be bused back to Washington D.C.

Needless to say Jack was very tired after this last mission, and he knew that at the end of the year he would be turning fifty years old, and he began to think of what life would be like sitting on the bright and sunny Daytona Beach in Florida. Once he boarded the passenger train, Jack went to the dining car to eat dinner before going to his room on the train to sleep.

The spy sat down at a booth and picked up one of the menus on the table. After searching for the right thing on the menu to eat, he waved for one of the waiters to come to the table to take his order. "Good evening sir. What would you like to dine on this perfect evening?" the polite waiter asked.

Jack intensely locked eyes with the waiter and told him his order of a medium rare steak and green beans with salt on them, and a fine red wine to drink since he was not on the clock with the federal government.

The waiter wrote down the order carefully and made his way to the kitchen car to help prepare the dish for Jack to eat. Jack began to stare blankly out the window at the passing mountains and reminisce about his last mission and what he will do once he retires to a beach home.

After gazing for a few moments Jack was jarred when the waiter returned not only with his glass of red wine, but also his medium rare steak and green beans. The green beans however did not have any salt on them. Jack, while being a hardened spy, still was kind enough just to eat the green beans.

The waiter told him if he needed anything else to raise his hand, and he will be right over. Jack thanked him for his dedicated service, and the waiter was on his way back to the kitchen car. Suddenly, a mysterious figure sat across the table from Jack as he was putting a fork full of medium rare steak in his mouth. "How are the bland green beans?" Lt. Dan asked in a menacing tone.

The hardened super spy with fifteen years on the job was shocked to see the three-legged arch nemesis of the United States sitting across from him on a train heading to Texas. Everyone knew Lt. Dan was the number one public enemy to basically the world, even the waiter knew this. Also the kitchen staff knew this, but they didn't know to put salt on Jack Spacer's green beans.

"What..what are you doing here?" asked the startled spy.

The three-legged cheetah cocked his head to one side and replied, "Well now that would be the question; why a genius such as myself would be heading to a place like Texas."

Jack knew that even within months he would be retired from the spy business, and he could then just relax but before all of that can happen, he was about to live out some of his most dangerous days.

The cheetah continued, "Simple. Once I get to Texas I can file the paperwork to run for governor of the state. Then it will help with my goal of becoming President of the United States, but before I can do all of that I need something from you."

Jack Spacer smiled a bit as he was a bit confused, but knew he was about to get the edge in the conversation.

"I need you to get me the GOV Codec File so I can win the governorship of Texas very easily."

Jack smirked, "What makes you think I will give you the one program designed to rig all election computers in a state just so you can take over the country?"

Lt. Dan looked right into Jack's eyes, "because if you don't I will blow up this train."

Jack saw the ice in the cheetah's eyes and knew that he would be crazy enough to do something like that; he had read all of the profiles on the crazy mystic cheetah afterall.

"Ok, ok, ok. First off, how do we find the Codec File?" Jack asked quietly.

With the same level of volume Lt. Dan answered him "You are the super spy, you should know how. I will be waiting right here in the dining car while you look for it."

So Jack went on his quest to find the GOV Codec File to spare the seventy-five hundred people on the train to Texas. He thought to himself, how hard can it be? There is probably only one of those on the train, and he was sure he would find it.Jack Spacer began his search in the cargo hold of the train. He had a government issued smart phone that allowed for the signal to be traced of the GOV Codec File. Unfortunately, since he was on a train, no cell phone service was to be had to call for backup.

His smart phone lead him to an orange backpack that was stowed away. Jack unzipped the front pouch of the backpack to find two USB drives. He plugged in the first one to his phone, and it revealed the GOV Codec File that Lt. Dan needed, he quickly removed it and placed the second USB drive into his phone. His phone began lighting up and playing disco music, he immediately removed it, but it gave him a grand idea.

The super spy returned to the dining car to sit across from his arch nemesis Lt. Dan. "Ok. I got the Codec Files. Call off the bomb." Jack said as if he were in a library. Jack handed the USB drive with the disco music to Lt. Dan.

"Not so fast. Let me try it out first." The three legged cheetah said.

Jack began to get nervous for the first time in years. Lt. Dan put the USB drive into his laptop, and it began to play disco music which mesmerized him momentarily. It was long enough for the train to pull into its destination and for Jack to call for back up.

"You are now going to be arrested for your crimes against humanity and common decency!" Jack said sounding like he had won.

Lt. Dan laughed and threw a smoke bomb and some firecrackers on the ground as he sprinted out of the door of the train to jump into his awaiting helicopter. "This will not be the last time you see me, Jack Spacer!" the cheetah yelled with a very high volume.

Jack knew he had won the day, but the war between Lt. Dan and the rest of the free world was not over, not by a long shot.

The moral of this adventure is: just when conditions warrant a quick response you must act tough and sometimes, not all of the time, but sometimes, that can be good enough.

Fire in the Form of Crystal Clear Fresh Water

This is the ultimate test according to my childhood friend, William Bakerski. That test would be: can you balance a quarter on the tip of your finger? While that may not seem exciting, it is in fact one of the most dangerous sports ever.

There have been five and a half deaths directly attributed to quarter balancing in the past seven years. The half death occurred when a contestant on a Louie Anderson hosted game show tried the balancing act, and it caused him to get cancer, so the quarter only got half of the credit for the cause of death.

Anyways, back to William Bakerski's Ultimate Challenge. He bet Charles NoLastName that he could balance a quarter on the tip of his finger longer. The bet was simple: whoever balanced the quarter longer won the ultimate prize: the other man's wife, children, and job, if he chose.

The challenge took place at the usual location: the parking lot of the nearest middle school. Both fierce competitors started by singing the Italian national anthem, as is customary for quarter balancing competitions. Then they began the competition!

The entire match lasted eight hours, sixty-seven minutes, and five seconds before William dropped the quarter off of his finger. He was quite upset, so it seemed. Charles was so happy that after finishing the customary victory dance, made famous by Ricky Martin, he cracked open an ice-cold beer, also a tradition. Just then, William informed Charles he had just won fifteen hundred children and five-thousand and six nagging wives, so, in fact, William was the real winner.

After a few minutes quickly going through the official Quarter Balancing Rulebook, Charles announced that he will forfeit the competition by using rule number 39 in the rulebook which stated: "Any winning competitor can forfeit the challenge by cooking the loser of the challenge a roast duck with all of the fixin's." So, in fact, Charles really did not lose anything more than a roast duck.

This story reminds me of a saying my crazy grandpa used to say, "If the French fries are too hot, then feed them to an infant. They don't know any better." Boy was he crazy.

Don't Jump to Conclusions They Might Trip
You

Once, back in the early 1990's, I used to run with a dangerous crowd. I will be the first to admit I did some things I am not proud of: from trying to cut a sheet of paper with a pair of scissors with the screw taken out of the center of it, to the disgusting act of trying to bake a cake without icing on it.

Anyways, this story is about the group of people I used to hang with and our groups' fearless leader, Steve. Steve had a knack for being well liked, probably because he had everything. A nice car, a nice movie collection, and a hot girlfriend; her name was Stacy, if my memory serves me correctly. We all knew that he was selling illicit materials on the side of having a decent job at the breakfast factory.

Whenever someone would ask how he had so much money we would cover for him by saying he worked on cars on the weekend, because in reality he was selling cartons of eggs to underage children. Now I know you must be wondering why eggs were illegal to sell to minors, but in the county I was living in at this time, they had a law that eggs must be purchased by a person over the age of eighteen on account of the amount of houses getting egged was very high annually.

One night, the whole gang decided to go out to celebrate the release of some new pair of pants released exclusively to the local mall. These pants were awesome because they only had one pant leg, allowing a constant cool breeze on your left leg. Anyways, the whole crew of: Steve, Donnie, Donnie, Donnie, Don, and I went to the local hangout called: *The Sweet Call of The Dynamite Warriors.* It was a bar that we all went to at least once a month.

The bar had been getting a lot of negative media coverage around this time because of their controversial games of Beer Chess. The controversy had been over the fact that no one every really won on account of their re-entry law. They had this weird rule that if you drank a soda, not a beer, you could bring one of your pieces back into the game. So anytime you lost a piece and wanted to get it back, you just had to drink down a two liter of soda, and bring them back in.

Well since there was a lot of media coverage of this controversial tournament, there was also heightened security. All of the police officers of the surrounding three counties were there as a matter of fact. Of course, since all of the law enforcement was at the bar; in those other counties it was absolute chaos: people were littering and blocking fire exits with empty cardboard boxes.

Our whole gang sat in the booth in the back corner of the bar/tavern/dive/stadium. There was a police officer who kept eyeing us while sitting on a barstool, holding a piece of paper. He stared at the paper for about ten minutes without looking up. Finally, he took his eyes off the paper, turned to the officer seated next to him and said something and pointed in our general direction.

Donnie also noticed what was going on and said, "I don't like the looks of this."

"Me neither" said Donnie.

"Yeah, me neither" Donnie said.

"That makes four of us." said Don.

Steve and I both just looked at the others and nodded in agreement. The officer got off his barstool and began coming our way with the paper in his hand. As he got closer, I saw a picture of Steve on it.

"You are under arrest for selling eggs illegally to minors." The officer said, as he got close to our booth.

"They did it." Steve replied pointing at the rest of us.

The officer replied "alright let's go." to the five of us as we realized Steve lied to the police and sold us out. The five of us went to jail because of that for the maximum sentence of one day for egg dealing, without a trial or anything.

The moral of this story is be true to your words, not anything else.

Wacky Food

I once knew a person who was a chef at a prestigious fast food restaurant called Tanner's. The chef's name was Tim I believe, no wait, never mind his name was Ranchero, that's what it was, how could I forget such a silly name? While all Tanner's served exactly the same menu, except for the Alaskan one that only serves fish, no fries, no chips, no drink; twenty four hours a day seven days a week. Oh, and of course the one that Ranchero worked at had a different menu too.

He was employed at the one in Kansas (there is only one Tanner's in each state, as per federal law). The reason why this one consistently won the Tanner's Favorite Son award each year was because of Chef Ranchero's signature creation: "bean fried beans with cold chicken nuggets wrapped up in a taco shell." People would come from all over the world to get a taste of the dish known simply as: "Tasteful Delight."

Ranchero quickly rose to become the most popular chef in Kansas, then the Midwest, then the United States, then all of North America! Television channels were offering Ranchero shows ranging from cooking shows, sitcoms, and even late-night talk shows, but Ranchero turned them all down, because he claimed he was just doing his job by making sure his customers enjoyed their food, and taking home his five dollar an hour paychecks.

It all came apart one day when the worst possible thing happened: Tanner's manager Felicity Hungerburger told Ranchero that he must either sell his dish's mysterious formula or be fired. Ranchero was flabbergasted when he heard the startling news that his one time friend and always boss had betrayed him. This news did not go over well with anyone.

Tanner's lord and master, which is what they call their CEO: Evan Sparkburger, was probably the most furious of them all. Not because Ranchero may lose his job, but because

Felicity's ultimatum had reached the news media. Evan was set to make billions of dollars by selling "Tasteful Delight" in supermarkets, convenience stores, and strip clubs. Sparkburger had to concoct a scheme to deceive Ranchero into accidentally selling the rights to his amazing dish.

By this time Ranchero was a poor man living in the storage closet of the Kansas Tanner's, because of his suspension from cooking, where he drank water from a mop bucket after he mopped the floor. In fact he grew so accustomed to it, he drank it throughout the day all the time. (Fun Fact: before Ranchero's suspension he actually tried serving the mop water with his dish until the fifth person who drank it died!) The CEO decided to meet Ranchero in person on a fateful day in early to late June, or whenever it was.

Sparkburger arrived in Kansas with his two very good offers. He walked into Tanner's and walked right to the back counter, "You

Ranchero?" He could tell it was him without asking because of the smell of mop water.

"Sure am." He replied.

The CEO told him his first offer, "I'll give you five-hundred dollars for the secret of "Tasteful Delight"."

"No, not for sale." Ranchero said in angst.

"How about this." The scheming CEO started. "I'll give you complete control of the Tanner's company…"

Before he could finish Ranchero started with, "Yes, and no take backs!" The CEO started laughing saying what an idiot Ranchero was that he could think that he now owned the entire company.

Ranchero called his lawyer Ralph, who I do not believe had a last name, who took the case to court. After months of deliberation a lip reader watched the surveillance tape and said, "Yep, Ranchero said no take backs."

The now former owner of Tanner's, Danny Tanner, stood up and yelled, "This is an outrage!" The judge told him to sit down, which he did quickly and quietly.

The moral of this story is that even if you think you can out smart someone never underestimate the power of fate. If you do it could cost you everything. Also, have a good lawyer on call at all times.

One of my best friends throughout my life has been, Tucker "The Ace" Bandit. Now, I thought he had a cool last name which struck up an interesting conversation when we were in elementary school; which is where our friendship began. For the time that I have known him, he has always wanted to be a racecar driver, not NASCAR or Formula 1 cars or anything like that, but more of challenging people at red lights to beat him to the next light.

Our story though, happens to begin much later than that, probably more like our college years.

As we grew older we did sort of grow apart; he left and went to Technical Collegeland and I started writing this book. So, one day, I reached out to my friend, Tucker, and asked if he would meet me for lunch one day when he was in town.

After a few missed connections, we finally met at a roadside diner in New Mexico. I sat down at a booth, waiting for my old friend to arrive, when suddenly the door flew open and in walked a man with a full beard, leather trench coat, and dark sunglasses.

He walked right up to my booth and said, "Is this seat taken?"

It took me a second to confirm that this was, in fact, my friend. Once I did, I smiled and pointed to the empty side of the booth to which he slid in and picked up a menu.

"I must be quick about eating," he said to me.

Before I could even say it is good to see you the waitress approached the table and asked us for our order. I had not even had a chance to look at the menu, much less decide what I wanted to eat.

Tucker said, "I will have two chili dogs, with no onions, fries, and a water to drink." He placed the menu back behind the napkin dispenser and started staring at me.

Since I was under heavy duress to decide what I wanted to eat, I started fumbling around with the menu, when all of sudden Tucker spoke up. "He will have chicken fingers and fries, with an unsweetened iced tea to drink."

The waitress finished up writing down the orders and headed back to the kitchen. I was still holding my menu and had a shocked look on my face, I am sure.

"I already know what you are going to ask me so I will make the following statements: Brian I am doing fine, I am working for the government, and I am a world class computer hacker." Tucker said quickly.

I always knew "The Ace" was good at computers, but I did not know he was good enough to be a computer hacker working for the government.

"How long?" I managed to ask.

"Bout seven years," Tucker answered quickly.

Tucker "The Ace" Bandit began telling me the story of how he was able to hack into the government's main computer and order a giant order of pancakes from Pancake Hut using a government credit card.

I found out he was responsible for the National Debt being so high in the United States, and the reason was he ordered extra syrup for all of the flapjacks.

Strangely, the food arrived very quickly as our waitress was back to the table with not only our drinks, but also his chili dogs and my chicken fingers.

"Wow that was fast!" I said to no one in particular, and therefore received no response.

Tucker, with the food in front of him, took his fork and ate four bites of his meal and stood up and said, "Sorry Brian, but I have to go. Official business, you know how it is."

I nodded as he walked toward the front door.

Suddenly, he turned around and said, "If you want to be as successful as me you must have: the courage of a champion, heart of a lion, and be as fearless as an eagle." He smiled, turned back around and walked out the front door.

I got up and ran to the window to see my long time friend leave, and as a saw him get into his twenty seven year old, beat up, hatchback, two door sedan, I knew I had been had. I knew that someone who is a master hacker for the United States government would not be driving a beat up old car. I was no longer in awe of my old friend, but instead frustrated because I had to now pay for the bill at the restaurant.

The moral of this story is: deceit is the most dangerous lie there is, especially if you get stuck with the bill at the end.

The Road Adventure to end all Road Adventures!

This story begins on a Monday. Both Jack and Michael T. Fox decide to go on a road trip to Arizona from North Carolina. They have both called in sick. Jack the pest control man and Michael T. Fox, who is not related to the *Back to the Future* star, but a different one that works at a car wash for baby strollers, so it is more of a stroller wash than a car wash. They figure it will take two days to drive to Arizona. So they pack up their winter clothes and mountain climbing gear. They also brought fifteen hundred dollars in pure gold to sell to the Native Americans in Arizona.

Then at five o'clock in the morning they set off to Arizona. About an hour into the trip Jack already wants to turn back around because he left something in his Radioflyer wagon at home. They circle back around and travel back to Jack's house where he picks up his loaded pistol stashed under his two year old child's toys in the wagon in the garage, after he retrieved the gun they were back on the road.

Fourty-one hours later they are driving through the Arizona desert, when all of a sudden Michael T. Fox starts seeing what he thinks are hallucinations. He sees Lt. Dan the three legged cheetah! The three-legged cheetah is running alongside of their 1985 Honda Accord, and Michael T. Fox, who is not driving, rolls down his window, "What do you want?" he says.

The cheetah replies, "Your souls or I'll steal your gold!"

Jack shouts, " NO Way! Take our gold!"

Michael T. Fox says, "No way, take our souls, they are useless anyway." Lt. Dan begins to wag his tail at extreme speeds, and after twenty minutes, Lt. Dan now owns Jack and Michael T. Fox's souls! Within seconds Lt. Dan vanishes and an Indian trading mart appears.

"We are here" Jack says. They both get out and walk up to a giant Native American named

Chief Inspector Gadget. Everyone greets each other with a simple "How." Jack begins to barter with the good Chief.

"We have fifteen hundred dollars worth of gold in the trunk of our vehicle, and we will sell it to you for twenty thousand dollars." The Chief takes a deep breath and replies "No." Jack starts to think about another offer but just decides to shoot the Chief in his old kneecaps.

"That's for World War I!" yells Jack. Michael T. Fox is unimpressed. Suddenly, a person looking just like award winning actor Sean Penn walks into the teepee, hands Jack a check for twenty thousand dollars, and he walks out, hot wires Jack's car and drives away into the sunset.

"What do we do now?" says Jack.

"How about we pray to our new God?" Michael T. Fox states. They both say a few words in French, and then Lt. Dan appears like a genie in a glass bottle.

"Head East and I will find you guys' transportation."

Jack and Michael T. Fox begin to head for the door Chief Inspector Gadget gets up from behind the counter of his teepee store, and he raises up a bow and arrow, "One shot, two kills." He says with vengeance on his Native American mind. He fires the biggest arrow in existence, and it sails right through Jack and Michael T. Fox.

Lt. Dan says, "Wow that was awesome." Then the cheetah jumps into a 1994 Power Wheels motorized Jeep, a vintage model, and drives away into his mysterious cheetah lair or cave or boat or where-ever he lives.

The moral of this tale is never get into a situation where you end up in the cross-hairs of a sharp shooting Chief.

Secret Societies in General

Yes, we have all heard the stories about secret societies and secret clubs. For example: rituals involving sacrifices of lamb and snake blood, corn-cob pipes, and old yearbooks to some pagan god that will allow their group of cult followers to rule the universe or something like that. Since I am a more positive thinker I would like to inform you about the secret groups that are out to do good in the world; such that a team of superheroes might do in a comic book.

The first group I would like to talk about is the Way City Slammers. Now, this group claims to be secret; however, they have formal uniforms made up with "Slammers" on the front and their last name on the back along with a number for each member similar to a button-up baseball jersey.

What does this group do you might ask yourself, or me, or whoever might be in a close enough distance to hear you? What do they do to contribute to a better tomorrow? Well, once a month, a group of highly athletic people meet in a secret warehouse to discuss the day. Midway through their meeting, they select five of the people who showed up who happen to display the most courage and dress the chosen five in matching basketball attire with the word "Slammers" displayed on the front. The chosen five would then search the city in their official van looking for a basketball court with at least five other people on it and challenge them to a game of basketball.

Once the game begins, The Slammers proceed to not play defense, miss every shot, and turn the ball over every other possession. By doing this it allows the team they are playing to beat them easily. They feel that by losing basketball games it allows people in the community to gain confidence and act positively; however, eyewitness reports mostly stated that the winning team would, a majority of the time, tell The Slammers how bad they are and how they need to quit playing basketball, but as the latest known record of The Slammers shows they hold a record of 0-134 with their last recorded game being July 14, 1999.

One thing I almost forgot to include was after every loss, each of the five Slammers players would tell everyone at the basketball court that day an important message, such as: "Kids remember to take your vitamins" or "Stay in school" or even "Hang in there kids, think positively and act positively". All good messages in my opinion but not at the right place or the right time as their audience was mostly people in their twenties who are either laughing in the Slammer's collective faces or shooing them off the court so they can play a real game of basketball.

The second group I would like to write about is a group called the "Don't Knows". Their sole purpose is to keep their passwords a secret. Each week, they meet at the same rental storage shed, and to be let in, one must recite the password. The passwords change all the time, as I have been told by a former member, who shall remain anonymous. Some of the old passwords range from one word such as "kitchen" to phrases such as "get off my lawn you rat!"

She told me once into the shed they had strict rules about what could be discussed, which pretty much limited the weekly discussions to talking about what next week's password would be.

The third and final group, I must admit I do not know much about because of their extreme level of secrecy and their lack of former members to interview. I believe the group to be called the "Jester's Club". This group's mission statement states that they must test everything to check for harm.

Published reports from researchers better than me have heard of instances of these Jesters trying dangerous things like making sure it is still not okay to stick a fork into a toaster, or seeing how heavy of an automobile it would take to run over your foot and break it, or how fast can you lick an envelope closed and not get a paper cut.

The group considers what they do a public service and publishes their six page reports they do on each thing they are testing in a bi-monthly magazine that is available at most book retailers.

So, in conclusion, secret societies have gotten a bad reputation recently with all the movies that have been made within the past five decades that show secret societies with blood-drinking, bacon grease loving, samurai sword wielding ninjas whose sole purpose in this life, as well as the next, in some cases, is to wreak as much havoc as possible.

The moral of these writings is: if you happen to have the misfortune of joining a secret society or secret club make sure it is one that does good things for the community.

Poetry Corner 3 Couplets

Deep Sea

You will never know how much you can feel alive,
That is until you take the deep sea dive!

Bug Spray

Please don't drink the bug spray
For if you do you will not have a good day.

Instant Rage

If you want to throw someone into an instant rage
Then all you have to do is throw them in a large cage

Happier Days

I would be having much happier days
If only I could be on the beach bays

Dangerous Shark

You ask yourself what is more dangerous than a shark?
That would be simple: a shark after it has turned dark.

Tackle Box Only in Case of an Emergency!

This is the story that made the town of Bakersfield famous. This story takes place in the 1970's, back when Jared Fogel was the all-time eating champion. Paddy O'McPaddington was a professional car driver. Not in the sense that he drove people around, but in the fact that if he drove by you, you had to give him a dollar. Let's just say he made a lot of money. No one was quite sure why they had to pay him money, but everyday they were told by him that he was a professional driver who needed to feed his family of seals fish each night.

That was until one day, in the middle of July, Jack the Artificial Man came to live in Bakersfield. Jack was not actually a robot or even created in a lab, but he was still referred to as the Artificial Man, probably for his love of the taste of deodorant.

Anyways, on this day in mid-July Paddy drove up to Jack and asked for his customary dollar, and Jack got so pissed that he grabbed the nearest thing to him, a fire hydrant, and threw it through Paddy's car window. He then proceeded to punch and kick all of Paddy's windows out.

When Paddy asked why he did that Jack pulled Paddy out of the car and threw him to the top of an eight story building from which he was never seen again. Some say he landed on top of the trampoline that is on top of the roof and spring boarded to the moon, but I know that is a lie because that is impossible. For that reason Bakersfield is currently the number one vacation destination for families of four.

The moral of the story is to make sure you check your travel brochure for not only historically accurate facts but also valuable coupons.

When a Skeleton Decides to Go Bad...

So our heroes, Hunchback and the Fat Kid, like any warm-blooded American were taking their two-weeks paid vacation. They were visiting the Beach Islands of Hawkland (the sun is not visible there on account of the millions of hawks circling the island every single hour of every single day of every single year since 1983). Unfortunately for Hunchback and the Fat Kid, their arch villain Billy Bones was also taking his two-weeks paid vacation at these very same islands.Our two heroes set up an umbrella and two lounge chairs in the sandy beach.

"Boy, I wish some of those hawks would scatter so we could get some sun." Fat Kid said.

"What?" Hunchback replied.

"I said wouldn't it be swell if these birds would allow us some sun by moving out of the way?" Fat Kid said with a little more power in his voice.

"What?" the elder member of the duo once again asked.

"Aww, forget it." Fat Kid disappointedly said.

Just then Billy Bones walked up to them on the beach.

Fat Kid saw him first and said, "What do you want?"

Billy replied, "Taking a vacation like the two of you."

Fat Kid felt provoked so he said, "Get lost will ya?"

Out of nowhere Hunchback says, "What is he doing here?"

Completely ignoring him Billy says with a grin, "I guess I will be on my way then." He starts to walk away.

"Good riddance." Fat Kid says in hushed tones under his breath.

As he is walking away Bones says, "I shall attack them while they are on vacation. First, I will feed the hawks tons of bird food, then they will become so full they will have no choice but

164

to poop all over my enemies parade or shall I say, vacation." He starts his evil villain laugh, but is interrupted when Fat Kid says matter of factly, "You moron, you only walked away from us by about ten feet."

"So you heard everything?" Billy Bones said meekly.

"Yes we did, I'll even bet my partner Hunch heard it too."

"What?" Hunchback asked.

"So you heard everything about the birds and the poop and everything?" Bones asked.

"Yeah!" Fat Kid said sounding like he just woke up to the aroma of breakfast burritos cooking. "We can do this the easy way or the hard way." Fat Kid continued.

"Please remind me again what the easy way is." Billy replied.

"The easy way is you turn yourself over to the police now and save us all a little bit of time." Fat Kid said with his new found feeling of confidence. "The hard way is you battle me and Hunchback in a game of Dance-Off 2000: the Arcade Game.

"I don't like either option!" Billy yelled as he started running on the beach to the nearest store to buy twenty-five thousand bags of bird seed.

"I hate when bad guys do that" Fat Kid said very tongue in cheek. "Time to catch this dirtbag!" Fat Kid yelled. Hunchback grabbed the umbrella and stood on the seat of the lounge chair. With a running as best as he could start Fat Kid yelled, "Ving, vang, voom!" and jumped on to the back of the chair catapulting Hunchback into the air which then hundreds of hawks grabbed the umbrella with their talons and quickly guided him over a running Billy Bones and dropping Hunchback right on top of Bones, knocking him out instantly.Fat Kid huffed and puffed while running to the scene of Hunchback sitting on top of a defeated Billy Bones. Suddenly a hand touched Hunchback's shoulder. "Great job, boys" a friendly voice said. It was Captain Caddywonkus who just so happened to be on his two weeks paid vacation as well.

"What?" a startled Hunchback said. The Captain and the Fat Kid had a laugh at the expense of Hunchback, completely ignoring his question, and leaving him very confused.

The moral of this story is: Without a doubt if you can, please take your two weeks paid vacation; however, if you do, make sure you do not waste it when your arch enemy takes his vacation to the same exotic destination.

These Cookies are Old and So are You

I would be lying if I told you that I forgot the time that my good friend, Tyler, and myself were traveling about, riding in his car with nothing to do, as most teenagers can attest to, when we decided to travel to the local mall. Now, this mall was a very popular hangout spot with all of the "cool kids".

It was called the Slumberdale Mall, but most people in the area referred to it as "The Slums" or "The Slum". It was unique because the food court inside of it featured a circus theme for all of the restaurants. If you had any fear of clowns at all, this was not the mall that you wanted to shop in, or at least not eat in. It was always surprising to me that any sane person would be able to withstand ten minutes of the same circus theme played over and over and over again on the speaker system.

Sure they had the regular chicken and pizza places that you would see in any mall, but the employees at these places were mandated to wear clown makeup and wear fuzzy red noses. It was quite frightening, actually.

Our story actually refers to Tyler and I and our visit to a place that was not in the food court, therefore not having to obey the strict circus mall food court order. This place was called Mr. Gandy's Dinosaur Cookieland, and let me tell you, they had the best cookies on the planet (that I have tasted so far). Each and every cookie was shaped into a prehistoric animal such as a T-Rex or a Pterodactyl. Some were chocolate chip, others were not.

Anyways, Tyler and I decided to stop into the mall and get some of Mr. Gandy's Dinosaur Cookies. Tyler parked his car outside of the food court of the mall (this was the biggest of the parking lots to the mall).

He said, "Let's just run through the food court as quick as possible, I don't feel like hearing that awful music."

I quickly nodded in agreement. We both got out of his car and made our way into the entrance, when something caught my attention out of the corner of my eye. It was two men dressed in suits and ties with briefcases. The only thing is that both of them had full clown make up on. Now you would think something like this would startle me, but I remembered about the clown themed food court, and thought maybe they had a business meeting or something today.

The two clowns in suits reached the door first as they walked with a brisk pace. One with blue hair and giant black framed glasses held the door for Tyler and me to walk through. We both quietly thanked him and made our way into the mall. As we did, two husky security guards stopped all four of us.

"Whoa, whoa, whoa, did you make an appointment to see the boss?" one of the guards asked.

"He better come out here, we have some important legal matters to discuss," the clown with the blue hair replied.

Suddenly, the glass doors to the right of us, that were painted to look like a circus tent, opened and another clown, this one with green hair and a nice dress shirt and tie, came out.

"What is the meaning of this?" The green haired clown demanded.

The other clown that came with the blue haired clown spoke up, "I am Bonkers with the UACC, and to my right is Bilbo Clownins with the AACC, and we have some questions for you to answer."

The green haired clown sounded offended, "What questions do you have?"

At this point Tyler and I were not going anywhere; we had to stay to see what was going to happen. Bonkers replied, "We were checking this mall's records, and apparently, you have license through the FACC to conduct business but not the UACC or the AACC. Explain yourself." (Later in my life I asked my grandpa what those acronyms meant to which he told me: UACC: United Association of Circus Clowns, AACC: American Association of Circus Clowns, and FACC: Federal Association of Circus Clowns.)

"Ok what kind of dues do I owe to the organizations?" The green haired clown asked.

"Adding up all of the late fees and initial fees for the UACC, you would owe us five dollars and an Elvis Pressley collectors stamp" Bonkers answered his question and pointed to Bilbo Clownins who also put in his two cents, "To license through the AACC you must travel to India and hone your elephant riding skills, and then send us a check for, I don't know, say fifty bucks?"

I could see the mall boss' temper rising, even through his clown makeup. "This will not stand!" he said in an outburst, "I would rather close this mall down than deal with the likes of you!"

Both Bonkers and Bilbo Clownins turned and walked out of the entrance from which they came. Tyler and I both had a good laugh about the situation as we headed to the escalator to take us downstairs to Mr. Gandy's Dinosaur Cookieland.

Not more than one week later Slumberdale Mall was closed down. Those clowns do not mess around I guess.

The moral of this story is: do not judge a book by its cover, do not judge a clown by his makeup.

The Tale of the Tape

The tape industry has always been known for the sticky situations that are created by their business practices. Workers in this industry have told me that they often times feel stuck in their situations, but since the pay was decent they were able to hold their families' finances together. I decided to investigate a local tape factory to find out more information, and as you will read in the following passage, there is nothing but lies and espionage involved.

I first made contact with a company we will call "The Tape that Binds" and I spoke with a nice receptionist that not only told me I was crazy for wanting to speak with workers and see the inner workings of a tape factory, but also that I was stupid for thinking people would care about the tape factory business, unless of course they made it their livelihood. So I slammed down the phone and decided it was time to try a different factory.

The second company that I contacted was "Aces of Tape" who were more than delighted with my request to check out their factory. I made an appointment to visit them the next Tuesday and wrote it down in my notebook. The days leading up to that Tuesday seemed like months, but when that fateful day arrived I was ready, or so I thought.

I arrived about thirty minutes early to the "Aces of Tape" warehouse located in the industrial section of downtown Oregano Falls.

I sat in my car for a few minutes, collecting my paperwork and making sure my tie was on straight. I knew that this would be my one and only chance to see inside of an actual tape factory. After making sure I looked my best, I exited my car to reach the front door with a front door man; similar to a bouncer you would see at a club.

I was a bit confused, especially when the burly man said, "Sir, it will be forty dollars to enter."

I was a bit frustrated, so I asked, "I actually have an appointment for noon."

The bouncer chuckled, "Ok, then it will be fifty dollars to enter."

I rolled my eyes, but due to my journalistic integrity I pulled a fifty dollar bill out of my wallet and threw it up in the air, and miraculously, it landed in the bouncer's hand. He swiftly opened the front door for me, and that is when the real adventure began.

The receptionist that I had spoken with on the phone, I had been informed, had been terminated for letting an outside reporter into their factory. Since I was there anyway, the new receptionist decided to let me go on a tour.

The first place we visited was the secret computer lab, where seated at his desk was their own payroll computer hacker.

The receptionist, Nora, informed me that he went by "hashtag" Nathan Parnes, and that he was one of the best computer hackers in the business. I wondered to myself how the computer hackers were ranked. Was there a monthly magazine dedicated to the subject?

The questions that were running through my mind were halted when "hashtag" stood up from his wooden stool and yelled, "I am the greatest!" Apparently he had successfully defeated the twenty-fifth level of *Ninja Fruit Slicer*.

The tour continued as we visited the lunchroom of the factory. As we entered the cafeteria, I quickly noticed the smell of old cheese and biscuits. It is an unmistakable odor.

Nora said, "This is where all of the workers eat, including the CEO and the janitor, who share a special table, and are served grapes on a platter." The other employees seemed to be eating hamburgers, French fries, and hotdogs which all are very common in a cafeteria setting.

After eating a pretty tasty hamburger and order of French fries, we moved our tour to the next destination. The next place we visited, and I was informed it would be the last, was the security office. Now I expected to see a desk or two with some walkie-talkies on it or something, but to my surprise it was filled with assault rifles, pistols, and grenades.

Nora quickly shut the door, and said, "Ok this now concludes our tour, but since you have seen too much already, I cannot let you leave…"

She started to reach into her apron pocket, why she was wearing an apron was beyond me, but her hand made it's way into the pocket, and I quickly ran out the door before she could finish her sentence. "Without fifty dollars to pay for your entry" Nora finished her sentence.

As I was driving away from the factory as fast as I could I came to the realization that the tape industry is full of lies and deception. The tour that I was on was just a smoke and mirrors event that proved nothing about the safety of their business practices.

The moral of this tale is: never judge a book by its cover; however the inside of that book may be deceptive as well so you probably shouldn't judge that either.

Mission: Deception

Back in the 1980's, the soon to be super spy known as Jack Spacer was given the assignment to infiltrate an international toy company, *Spirit of the Young Toy Company*. They were believed to be putting government secrets inside of some of the toys they were manufacturing. The United States government used its resources to land Jack Spacer an interview in the company for an entry level position. So he can begin what was believed to be a six year long investigation.

It was a Monday that Jack went in for the interview, so an unmarked police car dropped him off at the front door to Spirit of the Young Toy Company's main factory in Seattle, Washington. Naturally, it was raining.

Jack checked his pocket for the voice recorder and checked his ear for the earpiece that would have constant contact with him throughout the interview. Jack thanked the police officer for driving him and exited the car, which was heading back to the police station for further orders. Jack started walking towards the big entrance to the factory.

Once inside the massive lobby of the *Spirit of the Young Toy Company* factory, he was greeted by the front desk security guard named Carl.

"Ok, let him know you are here to see about an interview with a Mr. Snellsworth," the familiar voice inside his ear told him. The voice belonged to his partner, Richard Dellings.

Jack reached the front desk and reluctantly asked about his interview with Mr. Snellsworth. To his surprise, Carl smiled and said, "Right this way, sir." The burly security guard led Jack down a large corridor with many doors, finally settling on one with the name "Mr. Teddy Snellsworth, Human Resources" printed on it. "Here you go," Carl said as he politely held the door open for Jack. He could not see anything in the room as the lights had been apparently turned out in this office.

Jack Spacer walked into the dark room as Carl closed the door on his way back to his security desk. Suddenly a bright light, as bright as a semi truck's headlights, blinded Jack.

A voice could be heard, "Who are you, and what are you doing here?" it asked.

"I'm here for the interview," Jack said calmly.

The bright light stopped, and there was darkness for a moment. A normal office light came on and a small man in his late fifties was seated at a desk with two chairs in front of it.

"Well, please have a seat," Teddy Snellsworth gestured to the chair on the left side of the desk.

Jack sat down in the chair and reached out his hand to shake hands with the man in charge of human resources for *Spirit of the Young Toy Company*.

"Your resume is most impressive," Mr. Snellsworth started. "Why would you want to work at a toy company, much less this toy company?" he continued.

Jack thought for a moment, but the voice inside of his ear let him know exactly what to say: "Sir, I love toys. That is the most important thing to me."

Teddy Snellsworth grinned because he knew he had found his man for the job. "Congratulations, Jack, you are hired. I was very impressed by your references, several four-star generals and the president of the United States. How could I not hire someone that these people will vouch for?"

Jack was proud of himself for getting the job, because he did like toys, but he knew that it was only temporary on account of him being on a mission.

Jack Spacer left the offices with a sense of satisfaction that he was successful in the first leg of his mission. A car was there at the front to pick Jack up as he exited the *Spirit of the Young Toy Company* building. Richard Dellings was behind the wheel of the car.

He began his lecture, "Now Jack, I know that you love toys, but remember, my friend, this is a mission. I expect you to be professional on this one."

Jack knew what was expected of his behavior, but he was unsure of what his mission would be.

Richard continued, "What we want to find out from them is if they are putting government secrets inside of some of their toys. Now, I don't want to bore you with the details of what may be in their toys, but let me tell you, it is very confidential stuff."

Jack woke up the next day to find a note stuffed under his hotel room door. It read: "Come to the toy factory at 10:00AM." He quickly got dressed and had Richard drive him to the *Spirit of the Young Toy Company* building. Jack walked into the lobby and was directed by the security guard, Carl, to the first door down the hallway on the left.

Once he was let into the room he realized what was going on. Jack thought he would see people manufacturing the *Spirit of the Young Toy Company's* most popular toy, Captain Dad, but instead there were about a dozen people on laptop computers searching the internet.

Carl said, "This will be the first room that you clean, janitor," and he stormed out of the room and slammed the door on the way out.

Apparently, he had applied for the same job and did not qualify for it.

Jack thought he would dress impressively, so he wore his favorite suit and tie to work that day. Not a single one of the employees on the computer seemed to even notice Jack as he had a chance to look at all of their computer monitors to see what they were working on, and much to his dismay, they were all doing internet searches for government secrets.

This immediately set off an alarm inside of Jack's brain. He radioed to his partner Richard, and had him stand outside of the building as support. Jack Spacer yelled out, "FIRE!", but since he was the janitor none of the employees noticed or cared. In retaliation, Jack walked around the room and punched each of the dozen employees and picked up their computer, which he quickly threw out the window.

Richard was in the grass outside when the computers started to make their way down from the now broken window. Thankfully, Richard used to be a wide receiver for his high school football team and he caught each of the dozen computers before they hit the ground. Since he had driven just a regular car to take Jack to work, Richard called in the Backup Squad, who brought the government limousine so they could load all of the computers for research.

The Backup Squad also sent half of their squad into the building to arrest all of the employees. It was quite the scene as they also arrested the children testing out the newest toys.

Jack was made a hero and went on to complete many successful missions with the help of his partner, Richard.

Teddy Snellsworth was arrested after hiding out in his airplane hangar in the Midwest. He ended up getting sentenced for five years in federal prison for his part in stealing government secrets.

Carl the security guard was also put in jail, but he blended in so well, he actually became a prison guard. Now he can be found as the sergeant of a prison on the west coast of the United States.

The children who were testing the new toys were also arrested, but the judge was lenient with their sentencing and they were given a sentence of six years of a bedtime before eight o'clock.

The moral of this tale is: be careful of the toys that you play with; some may not be what they seem.

This story is about a friend of mine named Chance Howler. This guy was up for any sort of adventure that he could get his hands on; from waterskiing, to mountain climbing, to water boarding. I will never forget the time that he asked if I would raft down the Niagara River right on down the Niagara Falls, he told me it would be "the ultimate adventure." I informed him that I remembered the song from the group TLC, *Waterfalls,* and that I would have to decline to participate.

Chance set out to complete his journey to raft over Niagara Falls, but first he needed a partner to help him paddle his raft down the river and ultimately over Niagara Falls. Now if you have never been to Niagara Falls before, they actually have a museum of all of the vessels that made it over the falls safely (even though it is illegal), and also some of the crafts that did not safely make it over and had been crushed to pieces by the powerful water.

He set out to find his partner by doing what many other heroes have done before: walk into the woods in the hopes that a spirit will guide him to his rafting partner. Chance packed up all of his hiking gear and cigars and went on his way to the woods, but before going he needed to pick up a few energy drinks to keep himself energized, even though he would only be traveling a few miles on the river before the falls. He stopped at a Gas'N'Go convenience store.

Chance walked in through the automatic roundabout door and locked eyes with the cashier/owner Big Chief Walla Walla Walla, and he immediately knew who his traveling companion would be on this journey. Big Chief Walla Walla Walla was the bravest man in all of Southern Canada, but he had the unfortunate luck that his shift didn't end until five, and the clock read four thirty-eight.

Chance made his way directly to the front counter and said, "You, me, the Falls" while pointing at the burly Chief's chest.

"That shouldn't be too much of a problem, except I don't get off for another twenty minutes. Did you have any shopping to do while you are here?" The Chief asked.

"Yeah, I have to grab a few energy drinks." Chance replied sounding a bit disappointed.

"Partner, I will give them to you with a five percent discount." The tough Chief responded. This brightened up Chance's once solemn demeanor.

By the time Chance was done picking out his energy drinks and his beef jerky sticks it was time for Big Chief Walla Walla Walla's shift to end. The strong Chief jumped over the counter in one motion, and jumped into the passenger's seat of Chance's jeep. "Let us roll, my friend." Big Chief said as he put on his aviator sunglasses and pointed his finger forward.

Chance peeled out of the parking lot on the way to their adventure.

It took them maybe five minutes to get to Niagara River Park's parking lot, and Chance pulled the jeep into an empty spot. Out of the back of the jeep, the two adventurers pulled out a blowup mattress and two paddles.

"I thought we were going on a raft?' Big Chief asked, sounding confused.

"Where is the challenge in that? Plus if I need to take a nap I can." Chance somewhat joked. The two thrill seekers made sure the California king sized mattress was inflated to its maximum size, which it was (even though I have always known Chance to be an adventurous soul, he always thinks safety first). They put the mattress into the water and climbed on top with their two plastic paddles for steering, and before any police or sane person could stop them, they were on their way to one of the most dangerous things a person could do.

Their journey started out rocky as the mattress was taking all sorts of hits from the rocks in the water, plus the people on the riverbanks were throwing knives at them. Now the people throwing knives at them were just trying to get them to stop going down their river. Chance and Big Chief were waving to the people as the passed them by with their paddles.

Since these two did not realize how close they were to Niagara Falls when they set sail they both were a bit surprised to see the end coming up very quickly. Big Chief screamed a little bit to psych himself up for what was coming, and Chance laid down and fell asleep on the mattress. Just as they reached the apex of the waterfall Big Chief looked over at Chance and saw him comfortably resting on their mattress raft. He just rolled his eyes as they started making their way down Niagara Falls. Halfway through their descent Chance woke up and pulled the plug on their mattress causing it to deflate suddenly.

"Hang on Big Chief!" Chance yelled at the top of his lungs.

They each grabbed a side of the oversized mattress and jumped off thus creating a parachute effect with the deflated mattress. It allowed both of them to land safely on the tour boat that travels next to Niagara Falls. Coming to the stark realization that neither one of them new how to pilot the boat, they were left with the notion that the police would be catching them soon for breaking the law.

Chance and Big Chief were not wrong, as the Canadian police pulled up in a boat of their own to take the two to Canadian jail. Once captured they were each given two month sentences for going over Niagara Falls, but would have a court date for the more offensive crime of interrupting a tour.

They both were in a holding cell when Chance had an idea. "Guard, just to let you know I am an American citizen." The guard turned and looked at Chance, then to the police chief. "This guy is an American citizen, should we give him the regular treatment?" The police chief nodded, and Chance was released from jail and absolved of all charges.

The guard then asked, "What is your name big fella?" directed to Big Chief.

"Sir, my name is Big Chief Walla Walla Walla." He responded.

The guard's eyes seemed to double in size; he looked toward the police chief who nodded again. Since Big Chief outranks police chief he was also set free.

The moral of this tale is: while living your life you may have friends, acquaintances, co-workers, and classmates come and go, but someone who is willing to go on a great adventure with you, don't let them leave your life not even for a second.

How far can you Drive a Car?

Growing up in the city, the name John Wexler brings back fond memories of my childhood. No, John was no friend of mine; he was however the stupidest human being I have ever met. Late one night, my friend Jack "The Rat" Boxinton and I were walking down the dark city streets, and we saw John wearing his customary *Atlanta Falcons* football helmet. I ask, "What are you doing, Wexler?"

He responds by telling me, "I am cleaning the streets." as he repeatedly slams his head into a light post.

Of course you cannot talk about John without speaking of his brother, Donnie. His name was Donnie Wexler, but the whole neighborhood called him "Purvis", for reasons I still do not understand to this day. Anyways, he was actually pretty smart. Early in his life he was president of the "4-H" club at Martin Luther King, Jr. High School; however, once the

1940's rolled around he made the mistake of getting caught up running the Hitler Youth Movement at the school.

Last I heard about him was from my buddy J.C.D.X.A. who said that he, "Heard Donnie died in a cold water electrical fire." Whatever that means.

So, it is my opinion that their parents were responsible. To sum them up: their dad claims he shot JFK with a cannon from the Civil War, and their mother, well, she likes to collect Magenta colored crayons and melt them into clothes and purses.

The moral of this story is that if you raise your kids right then they turn out alright, but if you raise them wrong then both parents should be fined right around five thousand dollars to pay for the cost to the rest of society for having to deal with their children.

Don't Step into the Wild You Just Might Find Deadly Salmon

I used to know a guy named Chuck The Warrior. He was not in fact a warrior, but he was a game show host. His last name was The Warrior. On this day in 1973, Chuck was hosting the one-hundredth episode of the extremely popular game show, *Kill the Mice with the Fishing Pole!*, and as the show was just beginning taping, a contestant named Franklyn was answering his fifteen opening questions.

He knew that if he answered even one question wrong his pet mouse, JoJo, would be killed by Mary the other contestant. Chuck read the final question after Franklyn answered the first fourteen correctly.

He said, "The final opening question is: What year did World War II end?"

Frankly thought about it for a second and replied: "1975."

Chuck said, "You have got to be the craziest, stupid person I have ever had on this show!"

Franklyn then replied, "Was the answer wrong?"

"Of course it is" stated Chuck. "Mary, you know what to do."

The other contestant takes her ten foot fishing pole, swings it over her head, and the hook of it catches one of the claws of the mouse that is owned by Franklyn. The crowd begins to cheer very loudly. Chuck tries to quiet the audience, because as many people know mouse silence, or near silence is necessary, because of the dangerous elements involved. The mouse begins to fly in circles because it is attached to the fishing line. Spinning at speeds almost too fast to see, Mary decides it is time.

So with one hand spinning the rod, her other hand reaches for the knife on the Community Table, which she uses to cut the string causing JoJo to fly into the air and then into the hands of his owner Franklyn.

Chuck says, "You know the rules."

This meant that Franklyn had to now eat his own mouse. He nodded his head in agreement. However he made a sudden turn towards the door and began to run as fast as he could, but there were two of the biggest, strongest, and meanest security guards money can buy. The real biggest, meanest security guards are Walter and Jay at shopping center in Ashville, North Carolina but they are not corrupt so they work out of the goodness of their hearts.

The one thing the producers of the show did not count on was the two security guards being afraid of mice. So while they wanted to kill the escaping contestant, they were more afraid of the mouse he was carrying, so they ran into the corner of the studio like a bunch of sissies.

Franklyn made a quick exit, which of course made him a fugitive from the law. He jumped into his car and was quickly followed by Chuck and five of the biggest, meanest police officers in the world. There actually are five bigger and meaner police officers but they live in St. Petersburg, Russia, and this story takes place in 1973, which of course in that year there was not a way to physically travel from Russia to America making it impossible for them to appear in this story.

The chase lasted for five hours and ended at the most famous lake in America. Franklyn's car ran out of gas at the edge of the lake, as did Chuck's and the police cars.

Chuck said, "You've got to do it, man."

Franklyn tuned out what Chuck had to say because he knew the crime he was committing by not killing his mouse was punishable by fifteen years in federal prison. Franklyn decided to dive into the lake. As he did, Chuck jumped in after him, as well as the five police officers.

By this time the mouse had wrapped its tail around Franklyn weighing him down to the bottom of the lake, and since it is common knowledge game show hosts cannot swim; he drowned too, and the five police officers could not swim either, so they drowned as well.

The End

Sorry for the sad ending, but if it makes you feel better they were all bad people because they did not pay their taxes.

The moral of this obviously true story is to pay your taxes, but when you do, remember to write-off your mice.

Jack Spacer when he was a Racer

One of what has become one of his most infamous missions was when Jack Spacer was supposed to catch a counterfeiting criminal who loved racecars. On this particular mission, Jack would be going solo without the help from his friend, Richard Dellings.

When a mission was to be completed in the quickest amount of time with the utmost proficiency they would assign it to Jack Spacer, for he is known as a Superspy, which is a higher office than all other government agencies. He was assigned with the task of bringing to justice the worldwide money counterfeiter known as Luther Millionaire.

Luther Millionaire lived in an inconspicuous mansion in South Georgia; he knew he would be off of the authorities' radars by living there. The mansion was so incredible on account of the money waterfall that he had installed when he bought the place back in 1998. The money waterfall featured a constant flow of pennies, nickels, and dimes that formed a river that ran from one side of the mansion to the other, and into a reservoir in the backyard.

Luther was so rich, that he wore a tuxedo almost everyday of the year, except for Christmas when he wore a Santa Suit made of solid gold. He would go around the local neighborhoods and throw his counterfeit money out of his limousine, which was quite humorous since he bared a strong resemblance to Santa Claus.

Jack Spacer's cell phone rang as he was exiting a ski lift in Colorado, after just finishing a case of a crazy man who would intentionally knock people over as they skied by.

Jack answered his phone and was given his mission of catching Luther Millionaire since the government finally found out he was located in South Georgia. He reluctantly agreed, because he knew that going from a cold climate to a warm climate, especially quickly, often times caused him to catch a cold.

Upon stepping off of an airplane in South Georgia, Jack started to sniffle. He frowned that he may become victim of catching a cold. He was one of the toughest, most respected Superspies working for the federal government, but he could not stand to be sick.

He was greeted by his contact, FBI Agent Wilkins. Wilkins said in a Southern drawl, "Welcome to South Georgia!"

They shook hands and Jack Spacer nodded his head. "Let me show you where our headquarters is," FBI agent Wilkins pointed towards a small building next to the very small airport.

They both jogged towards the building to get off of the tarmac as two planes were scheduled to land in the next few minutes.

They entered a room filled with computers and not a lot of sitting room.

"What do we have so far on this guy?" Jack Spacer asked.

FBI Agent Wilkins thought for a moment then responded, "We know he counterfeits United States currency, he's located here in South Georgia, he loves fast cars and even faster women, and finally that he looks like Santa Claus."

The agent seated at a computer snickered as he was playing a game of *Ninja Fruit Slicer*.

Jack Spacer was thinking out loud, "Ok, we know this guy looks like Santa; have there been any Santa sightings recently?"

He looked at a newspaper sprawled out on the floor, another agent apparently loved to do the crossword puzzles, but only when seated on the floor. The headline read, "Santa Claus shows his presence to give out presents in February?"

Jack held up the front page, "Bingo!" was all he needed to say.

The next day Jack Spacer, FBI Agent Wilkins, and Agent Wilkins' trusty dog, Rover were on their way to the rich town of Auburndale. Once they arrived, they walked into the place where the locals have most of their conversations, the grocery store checkout line.

Jack grabbed a basket and put several loaves of bread in it.

The manager of the store saw the three of them enter and yelled from about twenty feet away, "Hey, dogs aren't allowed in here!"

Agent Wilkins and Rover left immediately, but not before calling Jack Spacer to open up a communications line so they could hear from the van in the parking lot. Jack took his basket and entered the first checkout line; there were two people in front of him.

"So what's this about Santa Claus?" he asked to either of the two customers in front of him.

The customer who was paying responded, "You must not be from around here." He finished his transaction and left, rudely.

"What do you think of him?" Jack asked as the other customer started to have his items scanned. The man turned to Jack and started speaking in a foreign language, most likely Italian. He paid his total and left too.

"How about you?" Jack asked the checkout clerk.

The young woman responded, "Sorry sir, I get paid to checkout groceries, not talk."

The manager of the store smiled and nodded as he was standing about ten feet away. Jack paid for his bread and walked out of the store disappointed.

He entered the FBI van and said, "We are getting nowhere with this Santa Claus angle."

Agent Wilkins nodded and Rover barked affirmation. "Where to next?" Agent Wilkins asked as he started the van.

"This might be a stretch, but I have an idea," Jack pointed to a racecar dealer billboard as they were driving by.

Agent Wilkins pressed hard on the accelerator, and the FBI van went as fast as forty miles an hour. They made it to the dealership just minutes before they were set to close for the day.

As they pulled up a salesman in a gray suit with a silk red tie started to rub his hands together thinking he was up for a big sale that was until he saw the big letters, "FBI" on the side of the van.

Agent Wilkins, Jack Spacer, and Rover exited the van.

"What can I do for ya boys?" the shady salesman asked.

Jack had a look of anger in his eyes, "First off you can tell me some information about this Santa Claus look alike," he pointed at the newspaper headline. "Second, you can tell me what you know about Luther Millionaire."

The salesman's expression changed from moderate to angry. "We here at Rich Guy Auto have a policy of not disclosing information about our clients" the salesman said.

Jack Spacer pulled a twenty dollar bill out of his coat pocket and held it out to the salesman.

As the salesman was taking the twenty dollar bill he said, "In that case, Luther Millionaire is the Santa Claus look a like, and he lives in that big mansion on the hill." He was pointing at a giant house on top of a hill in the distance.

"Thank you for your help," Jack said coldly as the trio climbed back into the FBI van.

Agent Wilkins drove as fast as the slow van would take them up the hill to Luther Millionaire's mansion. When they arrived there was an armed guard stationed in the front of the giant wrought iron gates that had the letters "LM" on them. The van pulled up the stationed guard.

"This is private property. Unless you were invited in, I can't let you in," said the guard with the nametag that read "Andy".

Agent Wilkins had a confused look on his face, "But your boss Luther Millionaire invited us in."

The guard, Andy, had an even more puzzled look on his face.

Agent Wilkins continued, "Yeah, he even said he would let Andy know so that he would let us in."

Andy the security guard shrugged his shoulders and opened up the gate. Agent Wilkins waved to Andy as he piloted the van up the driveway and to the front of the mansion.

Jack Spacer said, "I will go and check out the back of the mansion, you guys try to get in through the front." He opened the side door of the van and climbed out.

As Jack made his way around the side of the house, he could hear the roar of a starting engine.

Jack, fearing for his life, hid behind one of the giant trashcans off to the side.

A very fast racecar zoomed past and the afterwind knocked over all of the trashcans. Jack hurried towards the garage as the door was closing, and he slid under to find three different racecars stored in the garage.

Since Jack was a Superspy he knew how to hotwire any type of vehicle, so he found the one that looked the fastest and hotwired it to chase after Luther Millionaire.

Agent Wilkins and Rover were making their way up the massive stairs to reach the front door when a racecar driven by a man who looked an awful lot like Santa Claus raced past them and to the front gate. A few minutes later, another racecar, this time driven by Jack Spacer sped by. Agent Wilkins and Rover ran down the stairs and back into their van to try to chase after the two racecars.

Both Jack Spacer and Luther Millionaire drove past the security guard as he opened the gate for the two. The FBI van just cleared the closing gates as a frustrated Andy cried out, "You tricked me!" with his fist raised in the air.

Luther Millionaire and Jack Spacer's cars were chasing each other down the main roads, with Jack being right behind Luther the entire way. After awhile the FBI van was about thirty miles behind the two.

Their chase reached all the way to The Great Clay Field of Georgia, which was close to two hundred miles away from the mansion. Luther Millionaire's racecar came to an immediate halt as they were about to drive right off The Great Clay Field of Georgia as that leads to The Great River of Georgia. He managed to spin his car around and have his car facing the front of Jack Spacer's car.

Jack was not sure if Luther was crazy enough to drive straight into him, and Luther knew it was against federal government protocol to smash racecars in the name of justice, so they both sat there reviving their engines; waiting for the other person to make the first move.

Suddenly, the FBI van arrived, and Jack knew the tables were now turned to his favor. He also came up with a crazy idea, he put his racecar in drive and hit the accelerator, and before running head on into Luther's racecar, he turned and hit the car at an angle.

The impact flung Luther from his car, he was not wearing a seatbelt because Santa Claus does not wear a seatbelt, and as he flew Agent Wilkins opened up the van side door and caught the once flying Luther.

"The only plates you will be making will be license plates in jail," Agent Wilkins said with a smile, as he put handcuffs on Luther. Rover barked twice, and Agent Wilkins left the dog to look after the now in custody criminal as he went to check on Jack Spacer.

Agent Wilkins could tell Jack was hurt, "That was a brave thing you did."

Jack Spacer smiled and clutched his broken arm, "All in a days work for a Superspy."

They all laughed including Rover, but excluding Luther Millionaire as he was going to jail.

The moral of this tale is: if you are going to act like Santa Claus, do it one hundred percent of the time, not just fifty percent.

When I was about ten or twelve, I remember clearly, while visiting my aunt and uncle, the most important, life saving talk that I had.

It was a cold December night and it was around midnight, if I remember correctly.

My uncle says, "Before you go to bed I have something that I need to talk to you about."

Being a confused preteen I just shrugged my shoulders and continued brushing my teeth with peppermint flavored toothpaste. I spit out the toothpaste and said, "Alright, what do you need?"

He pointed at the empty seat across the table, and I sat down.

"Let me tell you about forests, Brian" my uncle said. At this point I was very confused. "They are the most dangerous places in the world," my uncle said very seriously.

I began to chuckle because all that I could think of was Smoky Bear and how to stop forest fires. My uncle stood there and pointed in my face, silently letting me know that this was not a laughing matter.

From out of nowhere he pulled out a chart that was hand drawn, poorly I might add, that illustrated his four points to why forests are the most dangerous places to be in the entire world. It literally had written in green and red crayon, "The Four Points to the Most Dangerous Place on Earth".

He began to lecture me on why forests where so dangerous, "First I must warn you about the wildlife living in those places. They include wild bears, wild cats, and wild ducks."

I had to interject, "Whoa, whoa, whoa, wild ducks?" I had a look on my face that was questioning his authority on dangerous places.

My uncle got a cold, stern look on his face; he said in a low voice, "Have you ever been bitten by a wild duck?"

Since I had not ever been, I had to assume that his point was valid.

"My second point about forests that I want to make is the dangers of the lakes that are often times at the center of a forest," my uncle was moving forward with the discussion.

I, being a "tough" preteen interrupted him by saying, "I don't think lakes are much of a danger to me, I am a really good swimmer." That was in fact true, because growing up in Florida means you have to be a good swimmer or an advanced level one depending on where you grew up in the state.

My uncle began to laugh, "Did you know that twelve out of fifteen people who jump into a lake in a forest do not ever return? Nobody is really sure of why that happens, it just does."

I must have looked confused because he continued, "Even people who jump in using a tire swing are not saved by the tire."

I just nodded and he continued with his presentation.

"This third point that I want to make about forests is their trees can be allies at times, but will turn their collective backs on you in a moment's notice; if it suits them," my uncle said cautiously.

I began to count on my fingers whether that would be a double cross or just a regular cross.

My uncle began to stare in my direction, "Let me explain: the trees can be good because they might keep some of the rain away from falling on your head, but they are also agents of evil when it comes to blocking out sunlight."

Now since I was born and raised in Florida, I had my fair share of sunburns before, so I had to question my uncle, "I don't think it's too bad of a thing if the trees block out some of the sun."

He looked at me with a sly smile on his face, "If you read the newspaper, you will constantly see stories about people who thought the way you did, until a family member or friend got sick and died from lack of vitamin D."

Since I was only a preteen, I did not in fact read the newspaper, so I had to take his word for it.

My uncle was hitting his talking groove just as he was introducing his fourth and final bullet point on the dangers of forests. "The last thing I want to tell you about forests, and the most dangerous, without a doubt is forest fires."

Now I knew forest fires were not to be messed with, because earlier in school I had read an article about the forest fires that were engulfing California's coast

. "Forest fires are so dangerous that movies are sometimes made about them. You know that motto about how you are the only person, who can prevent forest fires? Well it's not true. If you were the only one in the world who can prevent the forests from catching on fire, the world would really be in a tough place, since there are forests all over the world and only one you."

I knew he had a good point, but I don't think that's what the motto is meant to mean, however, I was too tired to argue at this point.

My uncle's eyes began to squint, "Let me tell you something, if you ever, ever see a forest fire in progress, you run as fast as you can away from it, there is no stopping it." He was waving his hands at this point.

I could tell that he was winding down on the lecture, when finally he said, "Okay, Brian, that is all that I have for you tonight. Now, get some sleep because we have to wake up early for the camping trip tomorrow."

I was terrified, but informed.

Meathouse Rock

I once was friends with this guy named Andre. We went back to being friends from grade school, as long as I can remember. The only problem is I have not seen him in years, but the last time I did it was an amazing adventure.

He called me up early that fateful day and asked if I wanted to go with him to grab a couple of beers at Shelly's, his favorite local bar. He also stated the band Hate Your Parents was playing a one-night only performance and the cover charge was only one bent in half quarter. I remember asking Andre "What is the point of giving them a bent in half quarter?"

"That is the way the world works." He replied with a new sense of dignity and life.

I arrived at his butcher block store called: We Love Animals, Trust Us at around seven. Andre said, "Good to see you but we don't close for another thirty minutes." I said, "Just thought I would get here early."

"Hold on one second," he replied "Last call for bacon to thaw!" Andre shouted across his small store. Suddenly there was a line of ten people waiting to checkout.

Once they had all paid, Andre locked up his store, got into my car and drove across the street to Shelly's. On the way there the most unbelievable thing happened. I saw a deer in the middle of the road. "A deer" was all that I could manage to get out.

Andre turned to me and said, "That's mighty nice of you to refer to me as dear." Then we hit the deer because he was driving and was not looking at the road, but since we were only going five miles an hour, the car and the deer exploded brightening the dark sky. I have not seen Andre since that night.

The lesson to be learned is to drive fast or your car will explode.

Things to Do, Things to See

Our story takes place in the home of Hunchback as he and his partner Fat Kid are sitting about in his living room contemplating what their next adventure could be. Hunchback was tied into his recliner with his hands holding up last Thursday's newspaper while Fat Kid was sitting with his back against the short table in front of the couch. Fat Kid was only a few feet away from the television screen as he was viewing an old wrestling VHS that his grandpa had taped for him back in the mid nineteen nineties.

Hunchback said, "Fat Kid, here is what we should do tonight since it is Friday night, and your mother has dropped you off here for the sixth night in a row. We should go to an auction to try to win me a new grandfather clock."

Fat Kid was seemingly ignoring Hunchback's comment about their plans for the evening. Hunchback continued, "Last time

223

when me and your grandmother went, God rest her soul, they had wrestling trading cards, 'betcha they would have them again!"

You would think they were giving away free doughnuts; Fat Kid rocketed to his feet and almost knocked Hunchback's prune juice off the table. "Grandpappy, you can count me in!" Fat Kid uproariously stated.

Hunchback smiled in delight and confusion, "First, there is one stop that we must make, and that is to eat dinner at Levy's Seafood. They have the early bird until five."

The pair was quickly on their way in Hunchback's station wagon down the road to get to Levy's Seafood before the early bird special ended. Hunchback was driving faster than he had in years, which was about ten miles under the speed limit. He knew that paying full price for a plate of Cod fish was unacceptable.

The trip was quiet until Fat Kid spoke up, "Can we listen to some music or something?"

It took Hunchback a few seconds to figure out what his grandson was talking about, but when he did his face lit up with a smile. "Of course! I have Frank, Dean, Sammy and a couple of other tapes that we can listen to."

Fat Kid just shrugged his shoulders and wondered to himself why his grandpa did not have a regular radio in his station wagon, much less satellite radio.

The blue station wagon pulled up to Levy's Seafood at four forty-five, which Hunchback considered prime dinner time. As Fat Kid helped Hunchback onto the curb in front of the restaurant, a beautiful blonde headed server opened the front door of the restaurant. "Welcome to Levy's Seafood." The hostess said with a smile.

Fat Kid winked and said, "Hiya babe."

The hostess rolled her eyes and asked how many were in their party. She quickly sat them at a table for two, as she could not stand the sight of Fat Kid's glaring eyes.

After a few moments of looking over the menu, a young man in his late twenties came to the side of their table, and delivered a basket of dinner rolls onto the table. "Hello, my name is Michael, and I will be your server today. If you have any questions about the menu please let me know. Our soup of the day is Chef's Special. Now what can I get you guys to drink?"

Hunchback looked up from his menu to tell the waiter, "I will have water, but do not dare give me lemon."

Fat Kid then spoke up, "I will have a Sprite."

After writing this down Michael asked, "Would you guys like a minute or are you ready to order?" Fat Kid just started shaking his head no. "Ok then, I will be back in a second with your drinks, let me know if you need anything else."

Fat Kid raised his hand. "I would like more dinner. What was your name again? Ah yes, Michael, I shall require more dinner rolls,

Michael." Hunchback just kept looking right at his menu without any shame or concern.

"Alright I will be back with your drinks and more rolls." Michael headed off back to the kitchen slightly shaking his head.

A few minutes passed by as Fat Kid finished the sixth and final roll as Hunchback was just putting the finishing touches on buttering his first roll. Michael was on his way back to Hunchback and The Fat Kid's table when his cell phone began to ring. Melissa, another server who was just hanging out near the kitchen as the grandfather and grandson were the only two people eating in the restaurant other than an elderly couple, who Melissa just had to check to make sure they were alive every fifteen minutes or so, jokingly said to Michael, "Oooh we're not supposed to have our phones on while on the clock."

Michael set the tray with the drinks and the reorder of rolls on an empty table while he reached into his pocket. "It's the boss. She is the only one whose ringer makes noise while I'm on the clock."

Melissa began to look worried; she knew it was never a good sign when the boss was making calls to her "employees". She picked up Michael's tray and brought it to Hunchback and Fat Kid's table. "Here you go dear. Michael will be right back to take your order," Melissa said to our heroes as she set their drinks and the rolls on the table.

"Wait, wait, wait, where is Michael?" Fat Kid asked annoyingly.

"I think he is back in the kitchen helping out our chef, we are a bit shorthanded." Melissa answered in a pleasant voice as she made her way back into the kitchen.

Fat Kid leaned over the table and said in his quietest voice, "I'll bet Michael had to make a big ole' poop."

Michael was off his cell phone and stopped Melissa in her tracks as she entered the kitchen. "You will not believe what she wants me to do."

He said solemnly. Before Melissa could ask he continued, "She wants me to kill Hunchback and The Fat Kid."

Melissa titled her head, "How do you think you will do it?" she asked.

Michael started ringing his hands nervously, he knew many have tried before to stop our heroes, but none have been successful, "Well I was thinking, depending on what they ordered, I would poison their food." He lowered his head and left the kitchen to take the grandpa and grandson's orders. "So what did you guys decide to have tonight?" he asked without any confidence.

Fat Kid went first as usual, "I will have a bacon double cheeseburger with tons of ketchup on it and no mustard. Oh, and double fries, and an extra side of Mac'n'Cheese." Without making eye contact with Michael he handed his menu to the waiter.

Hunchback was up next, "I will have the early special of Cod fish and a cup of your soup of the day."

Michael, as nervous as he was, did not remember that the Cod fish early bird special ended last week, and he took Hunchback's menu after he finished writing their orders. Michael walked back to the kitchen trying to gain enough confidence to do what his boss ordered him to do.

In between bites of dinner rolls Fat Kid was giving his grandpa the entire history of professional wrestling, and his grandpa was trying his best to not fall asleep before their order reached the table. Normally, Hunchback would fall asleep while his grandson was eating his second or third dessert.

Meanwhile back in the kitchen as the chefs were preparing our heroes' dinners by turning on the microwave to full power, Michael was busy gathering as much rat poison as he could find in the kitchen to put in our heroes' early dinners.

After a few minutes, Fat Kid heard music to his ears as the chef yelled, "Orders up!" Michael dashed to the two plates and one soup bowl and he put a little bit of poison in the ketchup on the bacon cheeseburger, and a little bit of poison in the Chef's Special soup. He loaded the three items onto his serving tray, and he traveled to the table briskly as his confidence was at an all time high. As Michael set the plates on the table he said, "Let me know if you two need anything else. I will be back to check on you both in a few minutes." Michael smiled and retreated back to the kitchen.

"Did you do it?" Melissa questioned. Michael just nodded with a disappointed look on his face.

Hunchback decided to eat his soup first, so he picked up his soup spoon and his arm shook so much that by the time he lifted the spoon to his mouth, there was not a single drop of soup on it. Fat Kid lifted the top bun on the bacon double cheese burger and said, "Hey, wait a minute. I didn't order any ketchup!" He followed up his outburst with a slam of his fist on the table; this caused Michael to return to their table.

"Is everything ok?" he asked.

Fat Kid was not happy, "No it is not, I didn't order any ketchup on this burger, and where is the mustard on it?"

Michael looked confused, "But you said you wanted extra ketchup and no mustard on it."

Fat Kid was getting really angry, "Are you calling me a liar!" he yelled. He took his left hand and pushed the plate as hard as he could off the table, shattering the plate and causing a very loud noise in the very quiet restaurant.

Out of fear, the woman at the other occupied table quickly pressed her Life Aware system that was on her wristwatch, thus calling for an emergency. Michael, trying to run damage control said, "I will tell you what, I will bring you two bacon double cheeseburgers to make up for my mistake."

Fat Kid, trying to hide a smile replied, "That will do, Michael."

Seconds later, the fire department broke down the back door that led into the kitchen, as just about the entire police department came in through the front door. Captain Caddywonkus walked up to the table that Hunchback and The Fat Kid were seated at. He smiled and said, "Hey guys, what's the big emergency?"

Fat Kid still had a disgusted look on his face and replied, "This waiter messed up my order and then called me a liar!"

The old woman at the other table gave the ok sign to the firemen who entered through the kitchen. "Which waiter was it?" Captain Caddywonkus asked, sounding concerned.

"It was that one!" Fat Kid pointed right at Michael.

Two burly police officers grabbed both of his arms and patted him down to find the rat poison in one of his pockets. They immediately took him to jail without any further questioning.

Melissa looked on as they hauled her co-worker off to jail and she vowed to get her revenge as now she was the only server and would have to work a double shift on Saturday.

Captain Caddywonkus was beyond ecstatic, "You boys have done it again! Is there anything we can do for you?"

Fat Kid only thought about it for a second, and then replied, "Actually there is something you guys can do for us."

A police squad car drove our two heroes through a drive thru for cheeseburgers and soup, and more importantly to the auction house so that Fat Kid could bid on an unopened box of professional wrestling trading cards from 2003.

If there is a lesson to be learned from this tale of our two heroes it is this: while things may seem to become impossible, there are always outcomes that can lead to making the impossible, possible.

Moose and/or Caribou Hunting Can Be Deadly

This is a tale of three cities: one to the east, one to the west, and one to the northwest. The three cities have no names; however they have one thing in common with each other, and that is they don't allow stray cats. The only way you can buy a cat in any of these towns is the Cat Liquidators.

Until one July 23rd. Old Jack Bankerkoffenberg decided that stray cats should be allowed in his town which was located in the east. The mayor William Pisserfacé, Jr. secretly thought it had the potential to be a good idea, but because the elections were so close, he did not want such an important issue to slip through the cracks of society. Especially since his opponent, Big Tex Dogman, was a very dangerous adversary.

Pisserfacé, Jr. put the issue on the backburner and put his re-election campaign as his main goal, after a short time of deliberation. Both candidates were very convincing during their debate in front of maybe twelve people, at best estimate. But as logic would dictate, there can be only one mayor.

One day later, it was time for the citizens to vote. At the end of counting all five votes the candidates were tied! Two people voted for Pisserfacé, Jr. and two for Big Tex Dogman, oh yeah, and one idiot voted for Captain Wallace Bambioffenclub for mayor even though the legend had passed away several years ago.

Pisserfacé, Jr. and Big Tex Dogman were forced to settle the election in the time-honored event of a sailboat race across the Indian Ocean. During their exciting race, both boats caught fire. So it became a swim to the finish. Since Big Tex Dogman had a five-thousand pound belt buckle on he threw it on top of Pisserfacé, Jr., and it immediately slowed him down.

Big Tex Dogman won the race and became mayor. He promised the town that his first act as mayor would be to send out a search and kill team to find Old Jack Bankerkoffenberg who may or may not be keeping stray cats at his house.

Within minutes a team of "experts" searched his home and found no sign of Jack or the cats other than a couple of turds on the couch. So now Old Jack Bankerkoffenberg has become the number one fugitive in all of the cities that don't really have names!

Little did the killing team know, Jack was fifteen miles away on a bicycle with an ice chest full of stray cats. Suddenly the chain on the bike broke in half, and the bike hit a chain link fence in front of a mound of burning tires. The ice chest flew fifty feet in the air and a good half dozen stray cats flew out. But don't worry, these crafty animals all landed on their feet, except for the Sandy because she has only two front legs and a chariot device for the back two. Luckily the other five cats flipped her right side up so that she could drive away.

Her fate was sealed when she was pulled over by a police officer of the law. He checked her license, registration, and phone records from 1995. After searching these items, the police officer said it was time to go, and he handcuffed her front legs together and tied them to the bumper of the patrol car and drove her back to the station where she was thrown in jail for the next five to twenty-five years depending on behavior.

The other five stray cats got away but were never heard from again, so they are all presumed dead by the National Guard. Old Jack Bankerkoffenberg ended up suing the bike company and getting several million dollars which he used to pay for a lawyer to clear his stupid name. He now lives somewhere with somepeople that don't really matter.

The moral of this tale is don't ride bikes ever especially if you have an ice chest full of stray cats or other undomesticated creatures.

Poetry Corner 4

A Rose in the Wild

A rose in the wild has no match for beauty

The beauty is non-existent unless you have seen
it

Once you have seen it you will never forget it

When you see it you want to tell everyone, but
also want to

keep it for yourself

The rose comes in many colors, shapes, and
sizes

Some red, some yellow, some white

Their differences are part of their beauty

But they are never mistaken for anything but a
wild rose

While many flowers try they always fail

The beauty of a wild rose cannot be matched

While other flowers seem to bring war

A rose in the wild has been known to bring peace

There are many flowers out in the wild

But a wild rose is the most elusive

They say that all flowers must wither with time

The wild rose does not

Our Heroes Return Part 2

We last left off with our heroes, Hunchback and The Fat Kid joined by the ever vigilant police Captain Caddywonkus in a standoff with Peter Excalibur and his henchmen, who happen to have several hostages inside of First Bank of the United States.

Captain Caddywonkus looked at Fat Kid who was about to explain his brilliant plan to rescue the hostages and thwart the plans of the evil Peter Excalibur. "My plan is two-fold," Fat Kid began to explain. "First, there are, what, seven windows to this bank?"

A police sergeant nodded his head to affirm.

"Ok, we will need fourteen pounds of cat litter, two for each window. We will then simultaneously throw it, shattering the windows."

The confusion was beginning to set in with the entire group of police officers surrounding the heroes.

"The second and most difficult part of the plan is: once the glass shatters and scares everyone inside, we rush in a combat team to take out the bad guys and save the good guys. I'll be home to watch wrestling at eight."

Captain Caddywonkus pursed his lips and tilted his head, "I have heard some crazy strategies in these types of situations, but this surely takes the cake…but if the past is any indicator, you boys have never steered me wrong."

A special combat police force was shamefully designated to go to the nearest store to buy a fourteen pound bag of cat litter.

Captain Caddywonkus received a phone call from inside of the bank, it was Peter Excalibur.

"Let me tell you something about these hostages: I will let half of them go, then y'all can leave and I will let the rest of the hostages go."

Captain Caddywonkus laughed hysterically into the phone, "There is no way that we let you get out of this alive, even if it means all of the hostages die!" The captain had not had his coffee yet that day.

Peter Excalibur was thrown into a figurative corner, so instead of doing the expected thing and surrender, he opted to stand his ground.

The special combat police force handed a fourteen pound bag of cat litter shamefully to their captain, even though he was still on the phone with Excalibur.

Captain Caddywonkus angrily cupped the bottom part of the phone and said, "I'm on the phone!" to his special combat police force, which quickly scurried out of the sight of their angry captain.

Fat Kid noticed the special combat police force and said, "Whoa, whoa, whoa, you guys bought one bag of fourteen pound cat litter, it should have been seven two pound bags of cat litter. I know I made myself clear."

Shamefully the special combat police force were now tasked with returning the fourteen pound bag of cat litter, and spending a few extra dollars getting seven two pound bags of cat litter.

The negotiations took a turn for the worse, as Captain Caddywonkus slammed down the phone in anger.

"He won't budge on any of our demands," he said in a frustrated tone.

The returning of the cat litter was not going any better, as the special combat police force leader Rodriguez was standing in line at the customer service counter behind a woman who seemed to be returning a full cart of groceries.

"Can you issue me a refund on a check?" the old woman asked.

The young customer service counter worker said, "Ma'am nobody uses checks anymore."

Rodriguez could see this situation was getting him nowhere fast, so he took matters into his own hands. He peered inside of her shopping cart to see just what he needed: seven two pound bags of cat litter.

Rodriguez made his move by pulling out his badge and saying, "I need to confiscate those bags of cat litter; it is an emergency!"

Rodriguez and his team partner, Donaldson, picked up the seven bags filled with two pounds of cat litter, and made their way to the exit of the store.

"Boy his cats must really have to pee," the old woman snickered before continuing her debate with the cashier.

"I think we are out of options boys," Captain Caddywonkus said to Hunchback and Fat Kid. He continued, "First off, Excalibur is not meeting any of our demands, and second, the Special Combat Police Force has not returned with the cat litter needed for your plan. I think we have no other choice but to let Excalibur get away with all of the money and the hostages."

Just as the embattled captain finished his defeated sentence, Special Combat Police Force leader Rodriguez and Donaldson walked onto the scene carrying the seven bags of cat litter. They did not use a grocery cart.

"No time to give up now, sir!" Rodriguez said with a smile. "We have come to the rescue."

Fat Kid smiled brightly as his plan was about to be enacted in a live hostage situation.

"Ok boys, here is what we are going to do" Captain Caddywonkus said, regaining some of his confidence. He had a map of the outside of the First Bank of the United States next to the police van. "I want to have seven men: me, Rodriguez, Donaldson, Stevie from accounting, Jenny from The Block, Hunchback and Fat Kid. We are going to position ourselves here, here, here, here, here, here, and here."

He pointed at the locations right next to each of the seven glass windows of the bank. "From then, on my mark, and not a second sooner, we will simultaneously throw the bags of cat litter at the windows, shattering them and causing confusion. I've taken the liberty to call in the

National Guard and the Salvation Army to be the first ones in to rescue the hostages and take out Peter Excalibur."

The plan seemed foolproof from the start, and the captain was now reassured it would work in these stressful conditions.

All seven were now in position waiting their command from the captain to throw the cat litter at the bank windows to cause a disruption.

Captain Caddywonkus yelled at the top of his lungs, "On my mark, three, two, one...throw!"

Six of the seven bags hit the bank windows shattering them instantly, and with the glass being so sharp, cutting open the bags and spraying cat litter everywhere inside the bank. The one bag that was not thrown was that of Hunchback's, on account of him not being strong enough anymore to lift the two pound bag of cat litter.

Fat Kid's plan worked out better than expected, because Peter Excalibur was in fact allergic to cat litter, so when the cat litter sprayed into the bank, he became blinded by his puffy red eyes.

The National Guard rushed in and captured Peter Excalibur and his bank robbing mates, while the Salvation Army stood outside and rang a few bells to attract the hostages outside of the bank to safety.

Peter Excalibur, knowing that his plan was thwarted, took his mighty sword and stabbed it through the tile of the floor of the First Bank of the United States where it remains stuck to this day.

Fat Kid was jumping up and down in excitement. "This feels like winning the wrestling world heavyweight championship!"

He began saluting into the air until, Captain Caddywonkus walked over to Hunchback and Fat Kid to congratulate them on their successful mission plan.

"You boys have done it again! I always knew I could count on the best to get the job done."

Hunchback smiled as he was proud of his grandson, "Fat Kid, I believe we are due to get some ice cream, and watch some wrestling, what do you think?"

Fat Kid nodded and started to shuffle from side to side, while clapping his hands together, not in any rhythm.

The moral of this story is: people always say to do things right the first time, but what if that doesn't work? Do you stop trying? Not by a longshot!

Deep in the Pacific Ocean, far from the coast of California, is a sunken boat called the S.S. Birchwind. Its story begins with its first and last voyage in 1998. The boat's captain was named Captain Richenburg and his first mate was named C. First mate C's first name was the actual letter and did not stand for anything, because his parents were hippies; however, C was nothing like them because he was a cat and not a human. Yes, he could talk and walk on two legs, so he was more of a hybrid kitty-cat.

The day started with a cold July morning on the ship, and Captain Richenburg was, as usual, yelling at all of his crew of seven. Apparently, the cook could not cook fast enough, and the farmer could not grow his boat crops fast enough either. The rest of the crew were just stupid so they got yelled at as well.

C was also mad at one of the crew who forgot to change out C's litter box in his office.

He started screaming at the crew too, but no one could understand him because he speaks in broken German.

Later, he sat down at his desk where his daily meal of dead trout is on a paper plate, but he is so mad C punches through not only the fish but the desk as well, and since we all know fish blood is an acid, it begins to burn through the hull of the boat, creating a hole that water begins to pour in from.

First mate C rushes to the side of the boat in time to see a hovercraft appear with Lt. Dan driving it. He tells C that he will give him a ride to safety in return for his soul. C has no idea what Lt. Dan said so the puzzled first mate picks up, carefully, the biggest, wettest sack of fish eggs he can find and throws it at the hovercraft, which expectedly explodes, sending Lt. Dan back to Hell where he belongs for the next four years.

C contemplates whether he should try to save the crew, but instead walks up to Captain

Richenburg, shakes his hand, and cuts him in half with his razor-sharp cat tail. He proceeds to call him a liar in what is believed to be German.

First mate C goes into the captain's office and takes the briefcase off of the desk, where he expected it would be. C's paycheck of fifty-nine dollars was inside of the briefcase. Realizing he needed to make a quick escape, because the rest of the crew was in the disco basement of the boat, and God knows disco will not last forever, C power walks to the aft side of the boat where the escape box was located.

Inside of the escape box was a pair of dice, which C immediately rolled on the top deck of the boat, and just as he expected not only did he roll two twenty's but that he also won his game of *Dungeons and Dragons*. After a quick fist pump, C dives into the water and swims for the coast of California, because it is common knowledge that cat-man hybrids are the best swimmers.

The lesson to be learned from this tale is disco, along with the crew in this story, are dead.

The Catskills Mountains Take All Skills to Climb Them

One day, in the early nineties, there was a group of adventurers who called themselves the Lords of Travel. That group consisted of Peter, Nancy, Jaborwa, and Luke. All which had their specific area of expertise. For example, Peter was their leader, Nancy was the medical expert, Jaborwa's expertise was his ability to navigate, and Luke was the equipment specialist of the group. Anyways, the group received a strange letter one day in their castle in North Dakota that read:

Dear Lords of Travel,

We challenge you to a race in climbing the Catskill's Mountains. The winner gets dinner paid for by the losing team.

Best wishes,
Sunnyside Travel Team

"I can't believe they are trying this again." Peter said to his team after reading the letter out loud.

"Guess ole' Dennis is at it again." Luke replied in his deep southern accent.

Peter thought for a minute then said, "I don't think it was him who wrote this one because it has the official Sunnyside Travel Team watermark logo on it, so I think it is legit." For the past seven months a twelve year old kid from Dallas, named Dennis, kept sending the Lords of Travel challenging letters, claiming to be several different traveling adventure teams.

All members of the Lords of Travel looked at each other with surprised looks on their faces because it had been five years since anyone had heard from their group after their last adventure to touch the bottom of the Atlantic Ocean.

"Do ya'll think it might be their boss Freddy Wifflestein trying to stir himself up some trouble?" Luke asked.

Completely ignoring his question Peter said, "Wait there is a phone number on the back of the letter, let me call and put an end to our speculations." As Peter was punching in the numbers on his cell phone Jaborwa interrupted with, "What if this is a trap?" Peter stopped, looked at him for a second, and then punched in the last number. One ring and the phone was answered.

"Hello?" said the voice that sounded like it was being awoken from a slumber.

"We just got your letter." Peter replied.

"Mom?" the voice on the other end asked.

"No, this is not her, but it is the Lords of Travel, and we accept your Catskills Mountain Challenge." Peter said sounding frustrated. Their was silence on the other end until a familiar yet dastardly voice said, "Glad you got our letter we are already in New York, the challenge is set for tomorrow at noon. Either be there or we will consider that a forfeit, and you will be paying for our dinners."

Before Peter could answer he heard a click as the phone conversation had ended. "We must prepare immediately for this challenge team." Peter said in a serious tone. "Jaborwa, call our travel agent, and book us flights to New York. Nancy, gather up our medical gear we will need, I will pack everything else, and Luke you continue to sit on the couch and watch the rodeo."

As the Lords of Travel all scrambled to get their assignments done Luke yelled out, "YEEHAW!" at the top of his lungs and threw his cowboy hat into the air hitting the fan which consequently fell out of the ceiling and through the glass table in front of the couch.

"That's Luke for ya." commented Nancy.

Several hours later the Lords of Travel arrived at the foot of the Catskills Mountains to be greeted by the Sunnyside Travel Team who was busy unpacking their climbing gear. Peter asked his team, "Anyone see the official Travel Team Officials?" (Every time two traveling teams faced off against one another, there had to be official officials because all of the teams did not trust one another not to cheat.)

"No, no I don't" Nancy replied.

Suddenly twelve loud sonic booms were heard by both teams signaling the entrance of the official Travel Team Officials. "I'll never get used to that sound no matter how many times I hear it." Walter, captain of the Sunnyside Travel Team, whispered quietly to his teammates for fear of the Lords of Travel hearing him and thinking less of him. Just then the officials were seen dancing their way to the challenge site; there were three of them doing assorted dances from the past three decades. They were dressed in their official's uniform which consisted of loose fitting black baggy pants and a tight white t-shirt with the letters TT in the upper left hand corner.

The competition was ready to finally begin as both team captains: Peter and Walter finished drinking their ceremonial two liter bottles of water. Sunnyside's manager Freddy Wifflestein shouted words of encouragement, "Come on boys! You can win! Put your minds to it!" All four members of each team were strapped into their harnesses, and the competition of climbing started once the head official shot the official revolver six times in the air, reloaded and shot it six more times in the air, on the last shot hitting a dove and killing it instantly.

All eight participants began climbing the mountains. Sixteen minutes into the climbing it began to rain making this competition much harder than either team had anticipated. The officials were actually discussing whether or not they should postpone the climbing, but instead they decided to make it harder by also making the team that reached the top slay the fire-breathing dragon that lives on the top of the Catskills Mountains. Their reason for the slaying being that the dragon owed several years of back taxes to the federal government and a bounty would be rewarded to them.

Freddy Wifflestein was furious. The officials got into contact with both teams. Upon hearing the news Peter immediately took control, "Situations changed." He said firmly. "Nancy I'll take point. The rest of you follow behind me."

Walter said to his team calmly, "This does not change a thing we will continue at our slow but steady pace and beat the overly confident Lords of Travel."

Unfortunately for them, it did not work as the faster moving Lords of Travel reached the top of the mountains first.

Now came the hard part for Peter's team, as they reached the top they saw a cave that had an entrance about forty feet high. "Nancy go hide behind that rock." Their fearless leader Peter said. Suddenly a thirty foot blue dragon walked out of the cave and said, "Hey guys what's up? My name is Eddie." In a thick Brooklyn accent and fire coming out of his mouth at the end of the sentence.

"Well to be honest we are here to slay you." Peter said not sounding too sure of himself.

"Ha! Ha! Ha!" the dragon replied, "No one in seventy years…" just then the Sunnyside Travel Team climbed onto the top of the mountain. All four ran at the dragon with clinched fists of rage. Just as they were doing this Eddie the Dragon spun around to see what the commotion was only to knock the entire Sunnyside Travel Team off of the Catskills Mountain, except for their leader Walter, as he was the only one to jump out of the way of the dragon's tail. "Blast!" was all Walter could yell as he watched his teammates fall off the mountain top only to be saved by their harnesses.

"Jaborwa go check to see if they are okay." Peter commanded. Jaborwa nodded and began down the mountainside.

"We need to stop this overgrown Alabama Lizard!" Luke yelled to his captain. He then jumped onto the dragon's tail, and it thrashed him about a bit until he was able to lasso the dragon's legs together tripping it up onto the ground.

Walter and Peter both ran to either side of the fallen dragon's massive head and said to each other, "on the count of three!" they both counted off out loud, and they both simultaneously flicked the back of the dragon's ears, thus killing it.

"Nancy it's safe to come out now, we have slain the beast!" Peter yelled cheerfully. Nancy leapt from behind the rock and stood next to the other three when they heard the noise of helicopter blades spinning as the three official Travel Team Officials were visible inside of the helicopter. They landed twenty feet away from the Travelers, and the head official announced that the four standing on top of the mountain were the winners: Peter, Nancy, Luke, and Walter. "But we aren't on the same team." Peter stated.

"As per official Travel Team rule six dash four one zero eight: if four Travelers complete a

task they must compete at least once as a team."
As the official finished explaining the rule,
Jaborwa and the rest of Walter's crew reached
the top of the mountain.

"But what about Jaborwa?" Jaborwa asked.

"Well, I, umm... don't..." was all Peter
could manage before an uncomfortable silence
filled the air.

The moral of this tale is: If you are on a great
adventure make sure you are in the right place
to get credit for it.

Contest of (Digital) Champions

Fat Kid's mom had to work on this particular Saturday so as usual she dropped him off at his grandfather's, Hunchback's, ranch style home. Fat Kid and his mom rang the doorbell to alert Hunchback that they were there.

After three rings the door slowly opened as the old grandfather was hunched over and he greeted his plucky grandson in the doorway.

His mother said, "I will be back at eight after my shift. You boys have fun." She turned around and got in her car and drove to another ten hour shift at the bakery.

Hunchback smiled as he asked his grandson, "What would you like to do today?"

Fat Kid, with a grimace on his face responded, "I want to go the video game tournament at the college today."

Hunchback shook his head and said with a smile, "Boy, don't you know the college is an hour away? We won't have time to go to that."

Fat Kid put on his best pouting face as he sat down on the brown leather couch and turned the television on to a show that featured wrestling highlights from the past week. Suddenly Hunchback's old rotary phone began to ring.

Hunchback shuffled over to the phone and picked up the receiver. "Hello," he said in a feeble old voice.

An ecstatic voice came from the other end, it was none other than the fearless police captain, Captain Caddywonkus, "Boys I have an assignment that I know, since you are both the best in the business, even better than us cops, will be best suited to accomplish. You see there has been word spreading around that there is a cheater in the midst at the video game tournament at the college. I feel with your worldly knowledge and Fat Kid's knowledge of videogames, you two would be perfect for the job."

Hunchback rolled his eyes as he knew that it meant that he would have to go to the video game tournament after all. He replied, "Only for you Captain would I be willing to do this; only if you really need us."

Captain Caddywonkus answered, "I wouldn't be asking you two if I didn't need the best."

Fat Kid had already turned off the television, and he grabbed his backpack as he knew they were about to go on another adventure. Hunchback on the other hand, hung up his rotary phone.

"Alright, Captain Caddywonkus just called and he wants us to go to the videogame tournament and stop a suspected cheater." Hunchback explained to his grandson.

"Whoa, whoa, whoa! We get to go to the videogame tournament after all?" Fat Kid asked almost rhetorically.

Hunchback just shook his head as the two heroes walked to the garage to leave in the grandpa's wood paneled station wagon.

As they were backing out, Fat Kid spoke up, "How long do you think it will take us to get to the college, grandpa?"

Hunchback immediately replied, "Too long." Hunchback was not too fond of driving on the interstate, much less in lunch time rush hour traffic. The pair drove in relative silence for the next hour as Fat Kid had his eyes on his portable videogame system, and Hunchback had his Perry Como cassette tape on but the sound was too low for him to hear.

The duo pulled into a parking garage on campus of the local college hosting the videogame tournament. There was a mechanical arm attached to a payment machine that blocked the entrance to the parking garage. The cost to park in the garage was five dollars for the event.

Hunchback was outraged, "Five dollars? Back in my day it was free to park your own car. If there was an attendant parking it, I could understand, but five dollars for me to park and walk all the way across the campus? This is insanity!"

Fat Kid laughed, "Grandpa, back in your day bread cost a nickel and television wasn't invented yet!"

Hunchback frowned and placed one of his five dollar silver certificates from 1896, which the machine promptly spit out. He put another five dollar bill in the machine from 1955 and the mechanical arm lifted up for the station wagon to enter the parking garage. Hunchback pulled out his handicap placard as the two pulled into a close to the exit spot designated for handicap parking only.

As Hunchback and the Fat Kid exited the station wagon, Fat Kid asked, "Is there any lead on who the cheating player is?"

Hunchback looked at his grandson with a confused look, "You are the reason Captain Caddywonkus wanted us on this case, because of your knowledge of videogames."

Fat Kid nodded his head up and down, "I see, so I get to be a detective! Cool!"

Hunchback smiled even though he hated videogames. The duo began their journey across the campus to go to the student center, where the videogame tournament was being held. Upon their exit from the parking garage they were approached by a student holding a clipboard.

The young man was obviously a college student and he went straight for Hunchback, "Sir, would you be willing to sign my petition to keep the wetlands clear from the college building yet another medical building? You would be saving countless animals homes and lives."

Hunchback held the clipboard in his hands for a moment before dropping it on the ground. "I don't sign anything; then your information is in the system."

Hunchback and Fat Kid walked away from a stunned and frankly, disappointed college student.

As they continued on, Hunchback felt the need to explain himself to his grandson, "You see while there might be some good causes that people try to get you to sign a petition for, they are paid by corporations to gather people's information to sell between each other. They just want to get people in the "great system"."

Fat Kid kept walking and for once did not have a comment for his wacky grandfather.

Our two heroes finally made their way inside of the student center as the competition was about to start. Fat Kid was amazed as national professional videogame players were in the tournament. He looked around the giant room to see on the stage, Ryan "Sticky Fingers" Webster, Jed "Richman" Richman, Tony "The Lion" Rodriguez, and many more recognizable faces. Fat Kid was in a bit of a stupor until his grandfather kindly reminded him of why he was here.

"Quick question," Fat Kid continued, "How can I get some of their autographs?"

Hunchback had a disappointed look on his face. A pretty blond haired girl handed both of the gentlemen programs to the day's tournament.

Hunchback came up with an idea. "How about you go up there and get their autographs, and while you are doing that see if you can determine who the cheater is."

Fat Kid nodded in excitement as he was about to meet some of his non-wrestler heroes. There was a giant clock on the screen that stated there was thirty minutes until the tournament was to officially begin.

Fat Kid made his way up on stage after showing the security his honorary badge given to him by Captain Caddywonkus. He walked up to each of the videogame playing professionals and asked if they would sign his program. They all were just happy to be there so of course they all signed.

When Fat Kid reached the last player on the stage, Jed "Richman" Richman he yelled, "This guy is the cheater, arrest him right now!"

The security team jumped up on the stage and arrested him. Out of the shadows came a familiar face, it was none other than Captain Caddywonkus. He also made his way onto the stage to help with the arrest.

"How in the world did you know it was him?" the Captain asked Fat Kid.

"It was easy, Jed normally writes right handed, but he signed my program left handed. If you look in his right hand you will find mirrors taped to it so he can spy on his opponents."

Captain Caddywonkus proudly smiled, "I knew you boys could pull this off. You both are the best!" Hunchback was sitting in the corner doing the crossword puzzle from the newspaper.

Captain Caddywonkus and Fat Kid shared a big laugh at Hunchback's expense.

The moral of this story is: always strive to go up, then you will never hit rock bottom.

Jack Spacer in: One Last Time

Once Jack Spacer reached fifty years old, he knew that his spy career was beginning to wind down. It was at this time, in fact, on his fiftieth birthday, that he began contemplating retiring from the spy game. He felt he had two options: go into spy management and continue living a somewhat spy lifestyle or write a book of some of his most exciting missions and risk being "retired" by current spies. Neither option sounded appealing to Jack, who just wanted to go fishing and enjoy his retirement.

He sat down with his friend and co-worker, Richard Dellings, who had already enjoyed a few drinks at the birthday party for Jack.

"Jack I think you are making a mistake," Richard warned his friend. He continued, "You are the best spy the United States military has, even at your age."

Jack Spacer nodded in agreement then replied, "That may be so, but I just don't know how much longer I can keep this up. I'm growing very tired of the spy game; I'm losing the passion for it."

Richard tried to reassure his longtime friend, "Here's what you should do Jack, give it one more year, then make your decision."

Jack had his response ready, "We're dinosaurs Richard. The technology has already passed us by, and by next year it will seem like we are used to abacuses."

The two sat quietly for a few minutes sipping their drinks and thinking in silence.

The silence was broken by Richard, "If you really want to get out of the business, I have an idea."

Jack perked up in his seat.

"The perfect time to get out of the spy game would be next month at the Annual Ice Cream Christmas Party."

The two longtime friends discussed over the next two hours how they would let Jack retire on his own accord.

What would be Jack's last month as a spy went by rather quickly as he plotted laying on the beach in Daytona and deep sea fishing in the Atlantic Ocean. The Annual Ice Cream Christmas Party started as it normally did with the chief of operations singing several Christmas Carols. Then for the next two hours there was a performance of *The Christmas Carol* which was followed by everyone's favorite part of the night: the serving of the ice cream.

The government was definitely not cheap when it came to variety as this year's lineup featured more than fifty-nine different flavors of ice cream. Some flavors were well known ones such as vanilla, chocolate, and strawberry; others were top secret flavors that have not even been named yet.

A few minutes into the ice cream portion of the event, Richard Dellings and Jack Spacer knew that their time had come to get Jack out of the spy game. They knew that no matter how much ice cream the government gets for their annual event, they always run out. So the two heroes hatched a plan to trick the higher ups at the party to let them go to get a refill on the ice cream, during which time Richard would say Jack had been captured by enemy forces.

The plan seemed flawless to them as Richard approached the chief of operations. "Hey boss, do you think that Jack and I could be the ones to go get some more ice cream from the store?"

The chief bounced his head from side to side, "Well that is Markum's job." He was right Deputy Chief Markum's job was to get more ice cream, which is what he was on the payroll for.

"Yeah but Jack just turned fifty last month and I know it would be the highlight of his illustrious career to be the one to pick up the extra ice cream for the party."

The chief of operations thought for a moment and said, "Against my better judgment, I will allow the two of you to be the ones to get the extra ice cream."

Richard smiled and nodded as he turned away from the conversation to gather his friend and go to get ice cream.

Richard Dellings was the driver of the unmarked government car, and his friend and soon to be former co-worker was staring out of the windshield of the car.

"Having second thoughts?" Dellings asked.

"No, not at all. Just thinking that we should get the ice cream so you don't go back empty handed to the party," Spacer answered.

Richard thought it was a good enough idea so they went to the supermarket to get the extra ice cream for the party. "I will just run in and get the ice cream so you don't show up on any surveillance videos."

After picking up the extra ice cream, Richard pulled the car over into the alleyway next to the grocery supermarket.

"Good luck my friend," Richard said with a tear in his eye.

"It's been real," Jack said with sympathy in his voice.

He continued, "You make sure the world stays safe."

They both smiled as Jack exited the vehicle and waved to his best friend and now former co-worker. Richard drove off back to the party, and Jack made his way into the shadows.

"They just took him; pulled him right out of the car." Richard said sounding terrified as he explained what happened to Jack.

The chief thought for a moment, "And where were you?"

Richard did not stumble at all, "I was in the grocery store checking out, in line with an old woman who was trying to get clearance for writing a check for ten dollars."

The story made sense to all of the government spy officials and they knew they would only have hours before the villains who took Jack would be out of the country.

Richard just kept thinking to himself, "Just lay low for a few hours, Jack, and then you will be free to enjoy your retirement."

Richard knew the protocol for searching for a kidnapped agent was that they had two hours to find a junior agent or in Jack's case three hours to find a super spy.

They did not find Jack in their three hour search window, so they gave up looking for the senior spy agent.

After lying low for a few weeks Jack made his way, just like he said, to Daytona Beach, Florida. He knew that was the place that he wanted to live out the rest of his long life.

The moral of this story is: there is nothing harder to do in life than to realize you need to give up what you are best at, but there is nothing worse than to not be able to do what you were best at in your top form.

The End

If you are reading this, then you have made it to the end of this book of short stories. I truly wish to thank you for reading this book and hope you thoroughly enjoyed it, or at least some of it, okay maybe one or two of them might have made you chuckle. If you have not read this book and just skipped to the last page in hopes of finding, I don't know, the about the author page or a glossary, well you are out of luck.

I really do hope that you enjoyed this amazing journey even as strange as it may have been, I can honestly tell you I had a great time writing this novel.

Thank you always dear reader,

B.A.G.

www.ingramcontent.com/pod-product-compliance
Lightning Source LLC
Chambersburg PA
CBHW031951040426
42448CB00006B/307